the art of imperfect action

Charis –
Take imperfect
action...

the art of imperfect action

ALL SUCCESS COMES FROM DARING TO BEGIN.

Allison M. Liddle

ALLISON LIDDLE CONSULTING, LLC
WAUSAU, WI

Library of Congress Control Number: 2018910507

contents

Dedication   vii

Testimonials   ix

Sign up for Allison Liddle's Newsletter   xv

Introduction   1

1. Be Empowered   7

2. Recover From Perfectionism   21

3. Using Failure to Achieve Success   41

4. Gain Self-Confidence   59

5. Jump—Don't Step—Out of Your Comfort Zone!   87

6. Set CRAZY Huge Goals   99

7. Finding Your Inner Magic   117

8. Productivity Hacks that Work   141

9. Crushing Self-Doubt: You are Worth It!   155

10. Go All In   167

11. What's Your Definition of Success?   177

12. Believe You Can and You Will   191

13. What's the Next Best Step?   205

Acknowledgments   213

About Allison Liddle   217

Works Cited   219

dedication

I dedicate this book to my little sister and brother, Anika and Reid. If you learn anything from your big sister, it's to take imperfect action and go after your goals and dreams in order to reach success in your life. There is no one else that is going to do that for you. Remember that it will feel a bit scary when you're stepping outside of your comfort zone. Take imperfect action anyway! All success comes from daring to begin. I believe in you. I will be here to support you. You are both world-changers, leaders, and are already doing so many amazing things to help others. I'm proud to be your big sissy.

Keep going!

I love you.

testimonials

Fear can be the biggest deterrent of our lives. Fear of unknown outcomes, fear of embarrassment, fear of failure. The Art of Imperfect Action helps you to overcome fears that you might be feeling and hurdles that you may have which are preventing you from becoming all that you can be. The steps and tools you find in this book will be your guide as you challenge yourself to fulfill your passions, your dreams, and your future. So, don't be afraid to read The Art of Imperfect Action, you just might transform from dreaming to achieving.

Kellie George (Nevada, United States), International Certified Communication and Leadership Speaker and Trainer

All successful people understand that practicing the art of imperfect action is the secret to achieve massive results. In this book, Allison walks you through the steps.

Jeff Rose (Tennessee, United States), CEO/

Founder of Alliance Wealth Management (alliancewealthmgmt.com), Creator of (GoodFinancialCents.com), Founder of The Online Advisor Growth Formula

The Art of Imperfect Action is filled with action steps on how to get started, how to 'get unstuck' and how to move forward in life. Allison's heartfelt lessons and examples from her life will inspire you, educate you, and empower you to take action in order to define and achieve your personal definition of success.

Ria Story (Georgia, United States), Tedx Speaker, Motivational Leadership Speaker and Author of multiple books (riastory.com)

The encouragement you need to step into the unknown is carried forward with gusto by Allison Liddle. This book will help you let go of perfection and move towards action. Allison encourages us to stop waiting for permission and just live because in daring to begin, we've already succeeded.

Laura Gallagher (Wisconsin, United States), President of The Creative Company (thecreativecompany.com), Wisconsin Ambassador for WED-Wisconsin (wedwisconsin.org)

Allison really gets it! She offers a fresh look at getting unstuck in whatever area of life this happens to be true. In a conversational manner, she simply invites to take small actions each day which invariably culminate into great changes in the end. Are you willing to join Allison on this journey? It is easy when you do it with someone – I have already said yes and I hope you will too!

Sarah Jessie Appiah (Switzerland) Former Member of the United Nations, Transformational Leadership Coach, Trainer and Speaker

In a very practical and real way, Allison has provided an excellent book including self-reflection questions and solutions to how perfectionism can hold us all back and how to deal with it so we drive forward to achieve our dreams and potential. Page after page I want to read on to uncover Allison's wisdom and as always I'm inspired and motivated by her positivity and wonderful attitude to life.

Joanne Hession (Ireland), Founder of The Entrepreneurs Academy Ireland (EntrepreneursAcademy.ie) and LIFT Ireland (LIFTIreland.ie)

What a book! Allison took a very simple statement

of "imperfect action" and transformed it into a journey that challenged me with things I wanted to do in my life but was afraid to start or push harder for. Thank you for the great lessons and stories you shared in this book that will push me to new limits in my life!

Ben Brookhart (North Carolina), CEO Power Home Technologies (www.pht.com), Author of *Success Hurricane*, and Keynote Speaker

I believe perfectionism is an excuse for our fear of failure, so we do not commit ourselves to launch. We are not born with a fear of failure. We are conditioned, after birth to fear failure, rather than being taught that all major, long-term success is fertilized with what we learn from falling, then getting up again and again until we succeed. "The Art of Imperfect Action: All Success Comes from Daring to Begin" will be valued for teaching that wisdom!!!!

Clifton Maclin, Jr. (Nevada, United States), President of Maclin International, Inc.

Allison's book "The Art of Imperfect Action" will help you push yourself outside your comfort zone to do more, be more and have more in your life! And she writes it in a way that is simple to understand. Read it, live it, and you'll transform how you live your life!

Deb Eslinger (North Dakota, United States), Executive Director of North Dakota Center for Technology and Business, Leadership & Business Consulting

I absolutely loved Allison's new book. Just like her previous book, "Life Under Construction", it was fabulous. Not only is it inspirational and packed with many beautiful stories that ignite your imagination and make you think, the book is a practical guide in how to overcome the burden of trying to make things perfect. Perfectionism is such a big problem that stops people from not following their dreams. The Art of Imperfect Action is a motivational "kick in the butt" that compels you to start taking action to achieve your goals and dreams. If you want to learn how to get out of that stuck place in your life, this is the right tool

Anna Simpson (United Kingdom), Confidence Coach, Inspirational Speaker and Author of *Create the Life You Dream About*

sign up for allison liddle's newsletter

Hello Friend!

Let's stay in touch. If you would like to sign up for my weekly email newsletter just sign up by visiting my website www.allisonliddle.com. In my newsletters, I share what books I'm reading, who I'm learning from, and where I'll be speaking or training.

Make today amazing!

Allison

P.S. Thank you for reading my book. I appreciate you. I can tell you're cool.

introduction

The problem with perfectionism is it becomes an excuse to do nothing. – Clifton Maclin, Jr.

Have you ever experienced analysis paralysis? I am the QUEEN of this, and one day I recognized that all of my analysis and over preparing weren't helping me get where I wanted to go. I needed to start taking action. But there was a little problem: I was a perfectionist. If you've ever met a type A perfectionist, you'll recognize the signs that I faced. I wanted to take action, but I felt like if I took action before I was ready, I would fail. I constantly criticized myself and had a terrible self-image. I just didn't feel like I would ever be prepared to go after the big dreams and goals I was chasing. Then one day I realized all of this perfectionism was keeping me stuck. I was stuck in my life. I was stuck in my business. I was stuck in my health. I was stuck in my relationships. I was stuck and I was sick of it.

So, what did I do?

I decided I needed to practice the art of imperfect action in massive ways. I decided to write my first book called, *Life Under Construction: Designing a Life You Love.* That was my first BIG imperfect action, and I remember feeling a bit uncomfortable throughout the entire process because I wanted it to be perfect. Even after hiring editors, having others read it, and reading it myself many times, I found an extra "s" on the end of a word after it was published. I realized something profound: it was the message that resonated with my readers. By taking imperfect action, I was able to positively impact the lives of others. After that book, I was addicted to taking imperfect actions both big and small. I started to push myself daily to take some sort of imperfect action.

I even traveled to Paris, France, to take the book cover photo as an imperfect action. It was a last-minute trip with my husband. Neither of us knew how to speak French, and we hadn't planned the travel itinerary. How often do we miss out on opportunities to do something absolutely amazing in our lives, but we miss it because we're stuck believing that we have to get it perfect? I've wanted to travel to Paris for years, but I thought I needed to have the trip all perfectly planned in order to do it. Guess what? I can tell you from experience that seeing the Eiffel Tower for the first time was an awe-inspiring moment for me. It's a huge structure, and it's much bigger than I had imagined. The first day when I saw it I was excited, thrilled, and determined to get closer to it. This forced me to walk the streets of Paris. To explore. To find my way. To take a journey. To have a huge goal on the horizon that I was taking steps toward. After seeing the history within Paris, I gained perspective on my life and how I was just living a small part of a larger story. Walking into the Notre Dame Church took my breath away and I felt the years of history, life, and death that were contained within its walls. I became aware of how precious this life of mine is and how it is part of a bigger story, a story that includes everything and everyone I meet. I felt connected to the people, the city of Paris, the culture, and the language in a very real way.

Have you ever felt like you were part of a bigger story? Have you ever felt connected to people you've never met before? Have you believed that you were going to do more with your life? Isn't this how it is when we are chasing a huge goal in our lives? We can see it on the horizon. You may not know all of the steps to get there, but if you take step after step in the direction of your goals and dreams, eventually you'll get there.

Recently, I started to speak to people all over the world and quickly found that a common fear held many people back in various areas of their lives. I found that they let the fear of not being perfect cause them to not try at all. Over and over I heard the same thing. People were fearful of trying new things because they worried that it would not be perfect. Guess what? We will never be perfect. You shouldn't let this fear of being imperfect hold you back.

Practicing the Art of Imperfect Action:

- The practicing day by day, month by month, year by year that a famous concert pianist did to become famous.
- The little actions my brother Reid and sister Anika took practicing their singing, perfecting their voices, so they could become amazing musicians.
- The jumping from the edge of the pool

into my arms, paddling, and then the swimming that my son Logan does now.

- The standing up, falling down, balancing, taking small steps, holding onto furniture, and then finally walking that we witnessed as our daughter Avery learned how to walk.

It's these seemingly insignificant imperfect actions that, day by day, month by month, year by year, will lead you to a breakthrough of magnificent proportions. The little actions lead you to something bigger and more significant because you've gained the experience you need to become the person you've always dreamed of becoming.

If you wait, without taking any action to become that person you dream of becoming, it will likely never happen. Thinking without taking action is doomed for failure. Thinking without learning, failing, and trying again won't allow you to learn the skills necessary to perfect your craft. Dreaming without moving your body in the direction of your goal will set you up for frustration.

The art of imperfect action brings together the little imperfect actions you need to dream bigger, learn more, and gain the experience to become successful. But first, you must begin.

All success is met by having the courage to begin. – Author Unknown

be empowered

Your time is limited, so don't waste it living someone else's life. Don't be trapped by dogma—which is living with the results of another people's thinking. Don't let the noise of other's opinions drown out your own inner voice. And most important, have the courage to follow your heart and your intuition. They somehow know what you truly want to become. Everything else is secondary. – Steve Jobs

I'll admit that for the longest time I did not focus my energy on being me. For the longest time I told myself that I did not have anything to offer the world. My self-image was negative and I was really good at pretending and trying to be what everyone else wanted me to be. Guess what happened to me? I felt drained of energy and unsatisfied. I wasn't being me; I was being someone else. That is no fun. Take my advice and don't do this.

My story starts about three years ago when I had my life go literally and figuratively under construction. Like a storm of destruction, my life was hit by the chaos of change. It started with having a preterm baby. I remember lying the hospital bed evaluating what was happening. I was three and a half weeks early, and that meant our baby was preterm. I prayed and hoped our little baby girl would be born without serious health complications. I have a background in early childhood systems building, so statistics flooded my head while I digested what was happening. The World Health Organization reports preterm birth complications are the leading cause of death among children under five years of age, responsible for approximately one million deaths in 2015 (Organization, 2018). Thankfully at 4:36 a.m. on May 24, 2015, Avery Hope entered the world, crying and healthy.

Shortly after Avery and I arrived home, my husband and I understood how critical great medical care is to the health of our children, and we put our home up for sale in northern Wisconsin. If you've ever tried to get your house ready to sell after living in it for over 10 years, you can understand how much work was involved. Add to that a three-year-old boy and a newborn girl. It was definitely not a small feat. We were shocked when the house actually sold fairly quickly.

Then we had to move to a new city and find a rental. This may seem easy, but it was not because the city we were relocating to had a shortage of rental homes. The funniest rental story I have is visiting a house that was located on a highway, had a pool table in the dining room, an oversized bathroom equipped with a bidet, boxes of clown shoes, and had fecal matter draining into the outside water feature. I can't make this stuff up. The prospects for rentals were grim, but we eventually found a beautiful rental home and signed on the spot.

During this moving and selling process, we were finalizing our plans to build a house. That brought a whole bunch of additional complications. When we finally started to build the house, the rest of the issues of home building surfaced. I refuse to allow them to make me upset anymore, so I won't share them, but it was not what we were promised, and the builder got fired. In the end, we now live in our wonderful new home.

We also decided to move the office for our financial planning business closer to our new home. This entailed looking for office space, building out an office, and branding the entire business. I don't know why we took on a second building project, but like I mentioned, our lives were under construction. Our office construction crew was phenomenal, once we found one, but it meant that we moved an entire house and office within about a month.

To top all of this off, I had a mole removed that had atypical cancer cells, and then I found a lump in my breast. The surgeon said we needed to operate to take out the lump. I remember walking into the surgery center that morning and feeling like I was dragging one foot in front of the other. I even asked my husband if I could just stay in the car. I thought if I ignored what was happening, it would go away. It didn't. I entered the surgery room sweating and afraid, but I knew I had to have faith. I needed to focus my energy on the lump being nothing. I decided to consciously focus on anything else while the surgeon operated, and I ran through a list of to-dos. I thought about my children. I planned my next fun family adventure. I thought about what I would do when I found out that it was not cancer, and I got my life back. I decided I would continue writing my first book. I would do more to help people live lives they love. I would start taking massive imperfect actions because I needed to do more with my life. When you're faced with your immortality, life becomes clearer. I knew I needed to focus on my family. I needed to help more people by doing things I'm gifted at, which is writing, speaking, and business building. A few days later the results came back, and it was not cancerous. I cried, I laughed, and I knew I had a lot of work to do. So, here I am living out my mission.

As if all of that stuff was not enough to handle, I received a call from my mom. She said, "Al, the doctors say I have breast cancer." I felt like I had been punched in the stomach. I could hardly breathe. My mom raised me as a single parent for most of my young life. If you've ever experienced cancer, you know it's a waiting game. You're diagnosed, and then you find treatments and a course of action. I was so afraid for her, and I was worried about what this would mean for our family. There were days during her treatments when I stayed at her house and helped her with my four-month-old baby in tow. I saw pain unlike anything I've ever experienced, and it was the darkest moments that taught me the most about how precious our lives are. I thought that I was invincible up until I had my own cancer scares, and then my mom went through her cancer treatments. I thought I had all the time in the world to do whatever I wanted to do. While I watched my mom literally fight for her life, I recognized how precious each day is that we are alive. I understood how critical it is for us to make the difference we were designed to make. I knew it was my mission to let everyone know that they have greatness within them, and if they waste it believing that they have tomorrow to take action, then shame on them. I had experienced firsthand the power in practicing the art of imperfect action.

After experiencing all of these changes, I needed to start doing something different in my life if I wanted to get different results. I decided then that I was going to put all of my energy and effort into creating a life that I loved. I wanted to empower myself and others. I wanted to lead a life of significance, not just success. I was going to start being myself, use my unique talents, ask for help, and put my life under construction.

Let me admit something to you. This was not easy. I've lived most of my life waiting for circumstances to be perfect before I took action. I thought one day I would magically have the time to write my first book or start my first business. I used to actually give myself excuses for why I couldn't start the things I wanted to do. When I was in my twenties, the excuse I used for things not going the way I wanted in my life was that I was just too young. Now I'm in my thirties, and I've come to realize that excuses are just false beliefs that hold us back from achieving what we were meant to achieve. If you want an easy fix, then this is not it. The steps I will be teaching you in this book are simple, but not easy. Once you read them, you will likely think to yourself, "Well, yeah, of course, that's what I should be doing." The trick is that many of the most powerful things that you learn in life need to be applied in order to be effective. They need to be acted on in order to work. Think for a moment about how many ideas, books, and trainings you have experienced. You may have said to yourself, "When I get done here I'm going to start ＿＿＿." Then you get back to the office or your house and do nothing with the wisdom you have gained. I won't lie, I used to do this all of the time. However, as I started to take steps to empower myself—steps which I'll share in this book—CRAZY things started happening in my life both personally and professionally. I'll share some of those results a little later.

After you learn more about who you are, you are able to start focusing more of your energy on the things that you're really good at. For example, imagine that you are not a very detailed person. You prefer seeing the big picture and working on projects that inspire you. However, you are working as a bookkeeper. Bookkeeping is more about details and less about big picture projects. But in recognizing this, you can figure out what your strengths are and align them with what you are doing in your career. Too many people are living lives they don't enjoy, and it's simply because they are spending too much of their lives worried about and working on the wrong things. A lot of us go through life without realizing what we are really, really good at. However, if we take the time for self-awareness, we can understand what makes us tick and use that to fuel our work and life in a positive direction.

Many of us live to make others happy or impressed. However, when we stop and think about it, all that does is drain our energy and cause us to be unhappy. I recently had my friend encourage me to start listening to my intuition more. I'll admit that I thought that sounded crazy. Now each day I listen more and more, and guess what that has resulted in? Awesome, amazing, wonderful, and unexplainable things keep happening to me. The more I listen and act on what my intuition tells me to do, the more my life makes sense. Take Steve Jobs' recommendation and start to follow your heart and your intuition to become who you truly want to become!

My main goal for this book is to *empower* you to do more, be more, and have more in your life by designing a life you love and practicing the art of imperfect action.

Empower (verb): to make (someone) stronger and more self-confident, especially in controlling their life and claiming their rights.

Imperfect Action: the act of letting go of perfectionism to take bold, courageous action.

Imperfect action is thoughtful action, but you take action, despite not having all of the answers.

Do you feel empowered in your life right now? The art of imperfect action involves simple, yet very powerful steps that you can take to empower yourself. The art of imperfect action can transform all areas of your life because you are moving boldly in the direction of your hopes and dreams.

The first step to empowering yourself is to BE YOU. More and more often we look at other people and compare ourselves to them. With the rise in the use of social media, this is increasing every day. Think about the many times you were on social media and thought to yourself, "I wish I had that person's life." Guess what is interesting about comparing your entire life to the highlights that someone else shares on social media? People only share the best parts of their lives on social media.

I'll admit that I don't share everything that happens to me. Recently, I was invited to Madison, Wisconsin, for a book signing at Barnes and Noble. Madison is one of my favorite cities, plus my little brother Reid is attending college at the University of Wisconsin-Madison, so it's great to meet him when I come into town. I brought a friend and my brother to get bubble tea, which I've had many times. I ordered and sat down, ready to enjoy it. When I stabbed the straw into the plastic top, the plastic cup cracked, and green bubble tea spilled all over my white pants, shirt, and my brother's backpack. It was not fun. But I laughed after my friend reminded me of the last time I had a book signing at Barnes and Noble, and I spilled a little guacamole on my shirt and pants. She said, "This makes the guacamole look like nothing, Allison." I did not share a picture on Facebook of the green tea all over my lap. And yet it happened, right? Think about all of the things you're not really seeing on social media.

There is only one of you on the planet, and you have unique personality traits, strengths, skills, and talents that only you can provide the world. You need to start thinking about who you are. You need to stop worrying about what others will think of you and start pursuing your passions. You need to start finding things that excite you and fill you up. You need to be empowered to take imperfect action.

There are people today who need what you have. And they are just waiting for you to find your voice so you can help them change their lives. – Russell Brunson

I've recently become the queen of imperfect action, because I have been taking massive imperfect action that has resulted in amazing outcomes and personal growth. I've had so many of my friends come up to me and ask, "Allison, what are you doing differently to get all of these results?" In the past year, I wrote a bestselling book, launched my speaking business, spoke to thousands of people from around the world, traveled over the equator with John Maxwell and his team to conduct transformational leadership trainings, and much more. I don't say these things to impress you, but to impress upon you that this process does work. It's not some theory I'm speculating. Some of my friends think that those results just magically started to happen. Those people make me laugh. The truth is that I started to take massive imperfect action, and I've gotten massive imperfect results. Does everything work out exactly like I hope? Nope. Do I wake up every day and just have everything happen how I want it to? Nope. Do I feel perfectly self-confident, strong, and able to conquer the world all day, every day? Nope.

But through my imperfect actions, I have realized that each and every one of us feel all of these ways at one time or another. Some of us are very self-critical. Some of us compare or judge ourselves against others. Some of us are fearful of change. However, as Karen Salmansohn said, "What if I told you that 10 years from now your life would be exactly the same? I doubt you'd be happy. So, why are you so afraid of change?"

In this book, I'm excited to share with you the steps that I have taken to take imperfect action and get things done. I've broken through my fears, pushed beyond my boundaries, and started to design a life that I love. I've learned how to help more people than I could have imagined and to move forward in life in an awesome way. I am very intentional in my ways of taking imperfect action and I know that you can do it too.

I believe in you. I know that there are areas in your life where you just need to stop thinking about things and trying to be so perfect, and just take action. I believe in you and know you're going to have amazing results! Then you're going to look back and say, "Oh my, why didn't I just start doing things like that sooner!" The whole point of this book is to help you start doing those things that you've been wondering if you should or shouldn't do.

Remember: Just do them!

Practicing the Art of Imperfect Action: Questions to Be Empowered

Each of us wants to be more empowered to design the lives we love. However, we need to start practicing the art of imperfect action before we can get results.

1. What would I do if I only had one year to live?
2. What excites and energizes me the most?
3. If I could do something all day long that allows me to lose track of time, what would it be?
4. What are my unique strengths? I would recommend taking a strengths finder assessment or personality inventory.

Your answers to these questions will start you on the path to being empowered to be you!

2

recover from perfectionism

Want to be happy? Stop trying to be perfect. – Brene Brown

I call myself a recovering perfectionist. The reason I call myself this is because for the longest time in my life I thought that I needed to look a certain way, act a certain way, and be a certain person in order to be seen as successful. Now I realize that I really was setting myself up for failure by thinking that way.

Have you ever wanted to be perfect in some area of your life? In reality, none of us are perfect.

Nothing is ever going to be perfect. The situation is never going to be perfect. You're never going to feel perfect. Trust me, the timing to start ____ (fill this in with whatever your next project is) will not be perfect. It's never the perfect time to start chasing your goals. Some of the best advice I have learned from mentors and through studying successful people is that taking imperfect action leads to success. All success comes from daring to begin. There is no perfect person, relationship, business, book, diet, car, vacation, or family. Doesn't that make you feel a bit better? I'm not suggesting that you be reckless in your decision making. It's important to make educated decisions and take action on big decisions and projects. I've made it a practice in my life to run my ideas through my advisory committee, which includes some of my close family members and mentors. They help me avoid wasting time and energy on bad ideas.

Once I had rid myself of the idea that I needed to be perfect in order to be seen as successful, I had an "aha" moment in my life. That's the day I recognized that I could start taking imperfect action. I could start doing all those things that I had been waiting on, things I had put off until everything was perfect. I don't need to have all the answers in order to just get started and take imperfect action. All I really needed to learn was how to practice trusting myself and my own decision-making abilities in order to move forward in a meaningful way in my life.

How many times in your life have you stopped and waited for everything to be perfect in order to take action? I know there are many people that wait their entire lives to take action in some area of their lives. Guess what? They never really accomplish anything. They get into their middle years or later in life, and they recognize that they missed out on so many opportunities because they waited too long. They waited for all those perfect conditions. One day this person wakes up and recognizes that life never turns out perfectly. There is not a perfect opportunity. I wish that opportunities came with a list of the benefits and negatives or that we had the ability to see into the future to see the outcome of making decisions, but this is just not the case.

I know that I was setting myself up for failure in many areas of my life with the idea that I needed to know all of the answers. I was doing it in my career. I was doing it for my health and fitness.

I was doing it with my family and in my relationships. I was doing it in my appearance. I was doing it in my friendships. I was doing it in all of these different areas, and it wasn't fun. It actually felt terrible. One day one of my friends pulled me aside and said, "Allison, I know that you're trying to be perfect. You're trying to hold it all together and be this perfect person all of the time. But, guess what? No one wants to be around someone that is perfect all of the time. Allison, you need to stop that. You need to stop trying to impress everybody. This person I'm talking to right now. You're being real and you're being authentic and you're being your true self. You're amazing. That is the person that I love and that is the person that everybody loves. When you're trying to be perfect, people recognize that, and they can see right through it."

I remember that day and how terrible I felt. I thought to myself, "Here I am, failing again." I lacked the self-confidence to be my authentic self. I lacked the self-confidence to show people who I really was. I had been telling myself stories for so long about how I was not good enough that I believed them. I was my own worst critic, and it wasn't good.

Today I feel so blessed to have this friend in my life. She had the ability to tell me something important which I really needed to hear. I still can picture her in my mind talking to me. That was a turning point for me. On that day, I found that I needed to stop worrying about what everybody else was thinking and just start taking imperfect action. That was the day I started recovering from my perfectionism. I needed to just start being myself and stop worrying about impressing others. I needed to intentionally surround myself with people who loved the authentic version of me.

Continuous improvement is better than delayed perfection. –
Mark Twain

For the longest time, I thought I needed to be the perfect wife, mother, friend, be in the best shape, have a master's degree, and do things perfectly in order to be successful. What this caused in my life was inaction because I was making it almost impossible for me to fail. In order to be successful, you have to fail and fail often. As I studied successful people, I realized the one thing that they had in common with each other was failure. They failed often. Then the successful people would use what they learned from that failure to improve and try again. It looks like this:

Failure to Success Equation:

FAIL > LEARN > IMPROVE > TRY AGAIN

FAIL > LEARN > IMPROVE > TRY AGAIN

FAIL > LEARN > IMPROVE > TRY AGAIN > SUCCESS

This process is often referred to as failing forward. If you are a recovering perfectionist like me, you need to stop it! In order to be successful in any area of your life you need to start failing and making mistakes. You need to figuratively get your hands dirty. Start taking imperfect action toward your goal. Staying in perfectionism mode only keeps you stuck.

As soon as you start working toward some crazy huge goal, it's likely that you won't "feel like it anymore." I've heard this excuse from so many people. It goes like this: you come up with a crazy huge goal that you're excited about. Then you start to take small actions toward the goal. Then you start talking to friends or family that can't understand why you would want to risk anything to do that crazy huge goal. Fear and doubt seep into you, and you somehow think that because you feel the fear and doubt that you don't "feel like working toward your goal." If this happens to you, I want you to ask yourself this question about whoever criticized your goal, "Do they have what I want?" Are they living a life that you admire? Have they accomplished a goal similar to what you've set for yourself? Are they leading a life of significance? If you answer no to any of those questions, perhaps they are not the best person to ask for advice. Think about it. If you want to get results, you need to learn from people that want the best for you. You need to surround yourself with brilliant people that are striving to be the best version of themselves.

Ask yourself: What is one imperfect action that I could take today toward my goal?

Six Steps to Help Recover From Being a Perfectionist

1. **Identify the areas of your life where you want to be perfect.**

I wanted to have a perfect career. I wanted to be seen as the go-to person in whatever industry I worked in. The funny thing about this is that I recognize that I have had a lot of different opportunities in my career that have all taught me so much. I would have never had these opportunities if I had stuck with my original "perfect" idea of my career. I know that I would have never become a serial entrepreneur. I would have never worked in a non-profit where I learned about leadership development and how to work in teams. If I had held onto my initial ideas, I would have never written this book! When you are looking at what you're doing in your life, you need to identify those areas where you have been trying to be perfect. In order to move forward and to take action, we need to have a clear picture of where we are in our lives.

Where in my life have I needed to be perfect?
– Is it in my career?
– Is it in my relationships?
– Is it in my family life?
– Is it in my health and fitness?

2. Discover your goal.

Later in the book, we'll work specifically on goal setting, but I want you to start thinking about discovering your goal. I'm letting you discover it because I know some people automatically will have a goal they are working toward and some people will not. Or, perhaps you've reached a majority of your goals and now you're trying to figure out what's next. Here are some questions that will help you discover the goal you'll be taking imperfect action toward.

– What is one thing that excites and scares me at the same time?

– What goal would give me the most fulfillment?

– If I chose one thing in my life to improve, what would it be? Why?

– What would an extraordinary life look like for you? Who would you be with? What would you be doing? Where would you be? How would it feel? Why is this important to you?

3. Believe in yourself!

Whether you think you can or you think you can't, you're right. – Henry Ford

Today I want you to really believe in yourself! Belief in yourself is critical to your success in any area of your life. I've actually written an entire chapter on this topic, but I want to introduce you to it now. If you start off already knowing that you are going to succeed, then you will succeed. When

I was at a low point in my life and I was trying to be a perfectionist, I did not believe in myself or my abilities. Each and every time I started anything new, I let ANTs (Automatic Negative Thoughts) in my head. Here is an interesting exercise. I'd like you to think about the worst scenario of chasing your goals and dreams. Imagine taking that risk and losing everything. You lose your house and your car and have no money left. What now? Are you destined to be homeless living under a bridge somewhere? I bet not. I bet that you would find a different opportunity. You'd find temporary housing, transportation, and hope. I bet that within a rather short period of time you'd be doing better than before. So, why is it that many of us let our fears dictate what we can or can't do in our lives? We let these false beliefs about ourselves and our abilities almost paralyze us. If you want to do, be, and have more in your life, you have to recognize the risks involved, make rational decisions, and then take imperfect action. I've found that most people do not believe in themselves enough to trust their ability to make the right decision. Most people ask others to help make their decisions, and many of the people giving them advice have not done what they want to do. Don't take advice from people who are not doing what you want to do and have received the results you want to achieve. It's much better to trust yourself and your abilities. You already know what you need to do. Believing in yourself means trusting your experience, your resourcefulness, and your abilities to do, be, or have what you want in your life.

4. **Take baby steps toward your imperfect action.**

One way to take imperfect action is to look for the low hanging fruit or the small idea that could move you forward in the right direction.

Ask yourself, "What is the next best step that I can take?"

What's the little stuff that you could do immediately to have some sort of result? Maybe it's as easy as writing that first email. Or perhaps it's just reaching out to that person you need to chat with. It could be setting up that meeting or signing up for a workout class. You may want to start marketing yourself for your new business. Just figure it out, whatever it may be. Many times, we try to set up all of the steps. I used to do it too.

I'd say, "Oh well, I'm not at this point in my project yet, so I can't take any steps." That was just my excuse to stay stuck.

I learned from my mentor, John C. Maxwell, that we find ourselves through confronting the problems in our lives. So, even those things in your life that seem difficult could be areas where you could start taking imperfect action. Maxwell taught me that you will never find yourself until you deal with that problem. Problems introduce us to opportunities. Opportunities are always surrounded by problems. It goes like this: problem>problem>problem>opportunity. The reason people don't seize the opportunity is that they don't want to deal with the problems. But in order to reach success, you must be willing to deal with the problems.

In actuality, you can start taking baby steps toward that goal—whatever it might be. Maybe you need to start today by doing some research or buying a book about the topic of your goal. Maybe you just need to figure out what that thing is that excites and inspires you. Sometimes when we are thinking about taking action, no matter how small, we automatically want to talk ourselves out of doing whatever "it" is. For example, you may have decided to start leading a healthier lifestyle and your first baby step toward that goal is to wake up early and workout. Let me tell you what probably will happen to you. You'll sleep through your alarm. Your dog will chew up your shoes. Your kids will be sick. Your treadmill will stop working. You'll have given yourself every single excuse of why today is actually NOT the day to start leading a healthier lifestyle because it seems as if the world is opposing your new goal. Do the one baby step anyway. Go workout. Do it. Each and every time you are trying to make a positive change in your life, you will be met with a struggle at first. You will have to overcome obstacles before it becomes a habit. Just understanding this is part of the process and is key to your success.

5. **Remember this is a process.**

Life is a process. Reaching goals is a process. Many of us overestimate what we can get done in one year, but we underestimate what we can get done in five or ten years. A step in the right direction, no matter how small, brings you closer and closer to achieving your goal. This also results in becoming a better version of yourself in the process. Many of us hold ourselves to a really high standard. When we are unable to lose 20 pounds in a month, have that seven-figure business in a year, or write a book in a week, we think we have failed. Success is built through daily actions. If you set your standards too high, then you tend to be paralyzed by the thought process. You may feel that you need to look like you have a certain type of life. What is the story you've been telling yourself that is setting you up to fail? Another good question to ask yourself is, "What do I keep telling myself is the only way that I'll be a success?" Taking it a step at a time means you are going to have those days that are great and have days that absolutely stink. I'll repeat: this is a process.

6. Am I listening to my true self or my limited belief system?

If you are recovering from perfectionism, you may have more challenges come into your life than you could've ever imagined. You may be tested. The perfectionism that you faced in your life could have resulted from your limited belief system or BS. It's that voice that says that you aren't enough and that you can't, you won't, etc, which as you're reading this you know is completely BS. But when the limited belief system creeps up when you're stepping outside of your comfort zone it's hard to recognize that it's BS because it's likely that you've never done what you're doing before. Unfortunately, all of us have a limited belief system. Some of us are better at recognizing it and identifying when it's impacting our thoughts. If you have a difficult time with comparing yourself to others or putting yourself down, you may be letting your limited belief system take a hold of your mind. The next time this happens, I want you to do this exercise.

I learned this from Oprah Winfrey, who was a successful talk show host and owns her own media empire called OWN. Oprah learned this from a yogi from India (Winfrey, 2015). The yogi asked Oprah to lie down and close her eyes. He said that he was going to say some words. He wanted her to imagine the objects and then let them go. He started, "Red triangle, moon, white-picket fence, etc." Each time you picture an object and let it go, you are actually recognizing the profound power you have within yourself. These are just thoughts. They are not you. This power will transform how you experience your thoughts. You have the power to observe the thoughts that come into your head and then let them go. If you are feeling negative thoughts, the next time one pops into your head, just note it and then let it go. Try this for one full day. At the end of the day, write down your experience.

How do you feel? I bet you feel more empowered. I know that the first time I did that exercise, I felt lighter and freer than I had felt in a long time. I recognized how often my limited belief system or BS was talking in my head. Your limited beliefs are that part of your self-talk that compares, judges, and offers automatic negative thoughts, and ultimately keeps you stuck. My BS was keeping me stuck in all areas of my life. With my health, it had me believing that I was overweight. I'm not; I'm stronger and healthier than I've ever been. My BS had me believing that I would not write this book. My BS made me believe a lot of false beliefs and stories about myself. I bet when you start to observe your own BS, you will recognize that your limited belief system is talking to you a lot. It may be sabotaging your best efforts. It may be keeping you stuck in your comfortable life. As soon as you stop believing the negativity to pursue your greatness, you'll have a breakthrough in your life. You'll start to have amazing life experiences. You'll start to serve the world in a huge way. Your life will inspire other people to write their own stories, to share their voices, and to become more of who they were meant to be.

Your true self is that whisper within yourself that tells you what to work on next. It is the voice that comes to the surface when you get really quiet. If you want to recover from perfectionism, you need to start to do things that will encourage your true self to emerge. Meditation, praying, and affirmations may help you reach closer to your true self. All that you seek is already within you. Many of us have a false perception that we need to find the answer to what we need outside of ourselves. In reality, we already possess everything that we need within ourselves.

When we fulfill our function, which is to truly love ourselves and share love with others, then true happiness sets in. – Gabrielle Bernstein

I believe in you. I know acting on your dreams may feel scary at first. Especially if you believe you can control everything. I was like that. One day I woke up and realized that I had held onto the false belief that I could control everything and I realized that I don't have that type of power. I needed to let go of all of those false stories and beliefs that were holding me back from becoming who I really wanted to become. My truest version of myself is perfectly imperfect.

Remember: You are perfectly imperfect and that is exactly who you need to be to be the truest version of yourself.

Practicing the Art of Imperfect Action: Questions for Recovering from Perfectionism

Imagine the best thing that could come from doing whatever it is you want to do. Close your eyes and see your life as the fullest, most successful version it can be. What would you have, do, or be? I've found as you start taking imperfect action on small things, you'll gain the self-confident belief in yourself to start taking action on bigger things. Build your belief in yourself by taking action and then figuring out what works. You are the person the world needs to do what you're dreaming about doing. You're now living a life that you love! Answer the following questions from that beautiful life:

1. Who could you help?
2. How would you make a significant difference in the lives of others?
3. What would life look like for your family?
4. Where would you travel?
5. Where would you live?
6. How would it feel to know that you now are living the life you imagined?

I'd encourage you to take a moment to write down all of the visions you're getting right now. These are the things that you are working toward. Your life is going to be better than you could have imagined. Believe you are the exact right person to have those things, do those things, and help those people. It's you!! You need to start with a little faith in yourself. You need to start small. There is a reason that you came up with the ideas. It's because you were the person that needed to go– after those goals and dreams. The world desperately needs more people to believe in themselves.

3

using failure to achieve success

In order to meet success, you need to work for it. You need to get out of your comfort zone. You need to try things out. – Allison Liddle

Successful people take action and then they fail. Then they get up and try again. Successful people know that in order to move forward in any area of their lives, they need to take imperfect action. Most people wait for perfect circumstances, and while they wait, they're wasting time. They are not doing what they need to do to learn what works and what doesn't work. It's an interesting predicament. You want to analyze what your goal is. You may want to have all of the answers before you start. But, in reality, you will never be 100% sure. You just won't. Time and time again, when I speak to my mentors, I realize that the one thing they are sharing with me is that they failed forward to reach success. They took the risks and massive action with having as little as 40% of the answers and ultimately reaching success. There is not a truly successful person on this planet that will say that they just sat around waiting for success to happen to them. I just asked my mentor, Clifton Maclin, about his views on failure and success, and he said he learned this from his mother:

The only failure is not acting with the intention and commitment to succeed. Excuses for not acting when acting was an option equals unforgivable failure. – Sarah Maclin

If you talk to any successful person, they will tell you that they've failed, and if they deny they have failed, they're most likely not being completely honest. I recently heard Jim McKelvey speak at Leadercast. McKelvey is an American entrepreneur that started over a dozen companies and was responsible for starting Square: Credit Card Processing. He explained how he started multiple businesses, and at the startup of each and every one of these businesses, he felt fear. As I started to research successful leaders, entrepreneurs, executives, parents, and non-profit leaders, I learned that people who are growing experience fear in some part of their life. If you are not growing, then you probably are not experiencing any fear. You will need to read the chapter called "Jump –don't step– out of your comfort zone."

Too many of us are not living our dreams because we're living our fears. – Les Brown

Fear creeps in when you are starting a new career or anything new in your life for that matter. As soon as you are stepping outside of your comfort zone, you will likely feel fear. When I started my *Life Under Construction* journey (moved to a new city, built a house and businesses), I felt fear all of the time. I remember when we moved to Wausau, Wisconsin, from northern Wisconsin. There were days when I literally did not know where anything was—including a gas station. I soon realized that I had been living in my comfort zone on autopilot for years. I decided that I needed to be intentional about growing in every aspect of my life.

Truly successful people have harnessed their gifts to achieve what they were meant to achieve. They're just doing what they're really good at and adding as much value as they can in the process. Eventually, all of this will lead to their success, either monetarily or as an influencer.

Interestingly, success is typically preceded by failure. However, the sooner you realize that you must first fail and then succeed, you are likely to reach your success. It's an interesting paradox. First failure, then success. I have a friend who hates the word failure. I asked him about the word and he said, "I don't like that word." "Why," I asked. "Because for my entire life I have been conditioned to think that if I failed, then I didn't reach my result, and therefore I'm a failure."

Too many of us have this perception of failure. When you fail at something, you may be saying to yourself, "I am a failure." This is completely false! Please, stop this thinking. If you are failing forward and learning from what hasn't worked, you are on the path to success. You're figuring it out. That's absolutely fine. I think that the sooner you can detach your self-worth from failure on your way to success, the sooner you'll reach success.

For the longest time, I attached my self-worth to the outcomes in my life. If I failed at something, then it automatically meant that I was a failure. If I succeeded at something, then automatically it meant that I was a success. Over and over again I played this false story in my head. What I've come to find is that truly successful people don't place the outcomes on themselves. If something doesn't work, it doesn't mean that they are a failure. It just means that it didn't work. What a concept.

Success is peace of mind attained only through self-satisfaction in knowing you made the effort to do the best of which you're capable. – Coach John Wooden

It's time to start thinking of failure in a new way, as a step in the process of achieving success. Most people do not understand this concept. They are afraid of risk, so they stay too comfortable, and they often miss out on amazing opportunities. Then they wonder why they can't reach the success that they crave. We all want to reach success. Our brains are actually hard-wired to want to be achieving goals. Even if you don't have a goal written down or a vision of what success looks like for you, your brain wants to help you achieve success! Isn't that awesome?

In *Psycho Cybernetics*, Maxwell Maltz, M.D, FICS, shares this: "... all of us have goals, whether we intentionally articulate them or not. The brain and nervous system are continually leading us in the direction of images we think about consciously, or images that are so much a part of us that we're led toward them on autopilot" (*Maxwell Maltz, 2015*).

What does this mean? It means that you must get out there and try things out. I've found that when I'm trying to figure things out, it helps me to find other people that are also stepping out of their comfort zones and surround myself with them. I need to know that there are other people that are uncomfortable too.

Now I anticipate change and I look for all of the amazing opportunities that could come from it. Rather than let fear cripple me like I had done in the past, I focus on the good and that allows me to harness the change for my benefit. I think all of that fear and change made it easier for me to handle change, and I've become more intentional about pushing myself outside of my comfort zone.

When your fear of failure bubbles up, take the time to recognize that the fear probably just comes from the nerves of trying something new, especially when you can't perfectly anticipate the outcome of your action. This is a good time to take a small imperfect action on the thing you are afraid of doing.

All of my mentors say you need to start failing more. When I ask them what is one thing they would tell their younger self, they say, *I would have risked more, trusted myself, and failed more often.* You need to start pushing the boundaries of what you've been doing in your life. If you aren't scared about something that you are doing in your life, then you really aren't pushing yourself out of your comfort zone.

Think into your own life. Pick one thing that you were afraid of doing. You probably worried about "it" and were overthinking it. But when "it" actually happened, was it as bad as you made up in your mind? I remember admitting to one of my supervisors that I would wake up worrying in the middle of the night about some of the stressors at work. I couldn't stop myself from fear, worry, and being anxious. I hoped he would have an answer for how I could deal with the stresses. He said,

"Allison, you can only control today. Why put negative energy toward tomorrow when all you can control is today?" That day I realized how much of my life I had spent fearing my future. I'd make up stories about how terribly the meeting would go or how something would not work out. I'm a fairly imaginative person, but I was using my imagination to come up with stories about the fears I was holding onto.

Guess what I decided to start doing? I told myself I would be present and stop worrying about tomorrow. If I was anticipating a change, I would say out loud to myself, "What if it turns out BETTER than I could have imagined?" This was a mindset shift for me because it required I shift from looking negatively at the future situations to looking for the positive in each situation.

When you are unsure about how something will work out, fear may hold you back, but don't give in.

My friend recently shared this from the book *You Are Doing a Freaking Great Job and other Reminders of Your Awesomeness* (Workman Publishing, 2015):

If at first, you don't succeed: Some of the world's most

accomplished people experienced overwhelming failure before finding incredible success:

- *Thomas Edison had about 10,000 failed attempts before inventing the light bulb.*
- *Dr. Seuss's first book was rejected by 27 publishers.*
- *Lucille Ball was known as the 'Queen of B movies' before landing her timeless sitcom.*
- *James Dyson created 5,126 failed prototypes for his bagless vacuum.*
- *Michael Jordan was cut from his high school basketball team.*

In order to be a success, you need to start striving toward your goals. There are so many people that are sitting on the sidelines of their lives and judging what others are doing or not doing. If they would take the time to take action on their goals and dreams, they would be surprised to learn how much work it is. It's kind of like how before you have children you feel like you know everything about being a parent. Then you actually become a parent and quickly realize that you know nothing about parenting! HA!!!

It is not the critic who counts; not the man who points out how the strong man stumbles, or where the doer of deeds could have done them better. The credit belongs to the man who is actually in the arena, whose face is marred by dust and sweat and blood; who strives valiantly; who errs, who comes short again and again, because there is no effort without error and shortcoming; but who does actually strive to do the deeds; who knows great enthusiasms, the great devotions; who spends himself in a worthy cause; who at the best knows in the end the triumph of high achievement, and who at the worst, if he fails, at least fails while daring greatly, so that her/his place shall never be with those cold and timid souls who neither know victory nor defeat. – Theodore Roosevelt

7 Fs to Intentionally Grow Myself:

Using failure to achieve success requires you to grow yourself. You can achieve a certain amount of success using only willpower. But willpower will eventually run out. I had a friend that wanted to overcome some major failures in his life. He had experienced crippling anxiety and fear and decided to start growing himself through personal development. He started to read and listen to books on how to grow himself to understand who he truly was. Through this process, he became more self-aware, and he also realized that many people faced the same fears of failure he had experienced. Many times, when we are in fear-mode, we blame the people around us for us feeling scared or fearful or we think no one else has ever felt the way we're feeling. However, the fear of failure is actually wired within us. In order to gain perspective over what is causing the fear of failure, you must grow yourself. No one can do this for you. You must decide to change and grow.

These are some of the areas in my life that I intentionally grow myself in.

Faith/Spirituality: My faith plays an important role in my continued growth. As I grow myself, I've found it helpful to stay connected to God by using these activities: daily devotions, praying, and going to church to learn and grow in my faith. Whatever you believe or not believe is fine. I just wanted to share what I've found helpful in my life.

Family: I place a high value on my family. I know that by focusing on loving and supporting my family, my heart will be filled with happiness. My family members are the most important people in my life, and I've found that prioritizing quality time with them has helped me grow. My children, husband, mom, step-dad, brother, and sister are my favorite people, and after I spend time with them, I feel better about myself. I also have an amazing extended family, and I know that they love and support me. I know that many people don't have a family like this, so I feel very blessed to know that I do.

Fitness: For a long time, I did not find time to exercise. I gave myself excuses for why I shouldn't be healthy. During this time, I felt anxious all of the time and I felt terrible about myself. After my children were born, I made the goal to live to be 150 years old, and in order to do this, I needed to intentionally keep my mind, body, and spirit healthy. It is now a priority in my life every day.

Finances: Money was always a taboo subject as I was growing up. Thankfully, my Grandpa Paul and Grandma Agnes were committed to educating me about saving money and spending money. I'm so grateful they shared their money mindset with me from a very young age. In order to grow myself, I need to have control of my finances. I need to understand where my money is and what goals I have financially. Now my husband and I own a financial planning company called Prosper Wealth Management (www.prosperwealth.com), so we see the critical importance of getting your financial life in order.

Field/Career: How many people despise their career? Unfortunately, as I speak to more and more people, I find that this is the case with too many people. It makes me remember the time when I felt stuck in my professional life. I was doing the things that I thought I needed to do in order to be seen as successful, but I was not getting the results that I needed and wanted. I was frustrated, angry, and I blamed everyone else for why I "had to" do that. Guess what? If I am not happy in my career, I have a choice to make: either stay with it or change it. It's really quite simple.

Everything you do is based on the choices you make. It's not your parents, your past relationships, your job, the economy, the weather, an argument, or your age that is to blame. You and only you are responsible for every decision you make. Period. – Author Unknown

It is up to each and every one of us to make a

change. Don't waste the majority of your life in a career that you despise. It'll drain your energy. Look for a career that excites and inspires you. If you don't know what it is, start exploring new opportunities.

Friends: Surround yourself with those who lift you higher. Many people stay with the same friends that they have had since high school. I have one really good friend from high school—oh, and I married another one! Besides those two, I've found that I have outgrown most of my relationships from high school. I'm not better than my high school friends, I'm just on a different path than they are. I've also realized that I need different friends for different functions in my life. I would suggest that you write a list of your closest friends and then put a (+) or a (-) next to each name depending on how you feel when you are with them. When you are intentionally growing yourself, I suggest you focus your time on the friends that are (+) and limit your time with the friends that are (-). Successful people are friends with other successful people. Who you surround yourself with is important to your success.

Fun: When I was in college I received a card from my mom that said, "There is not a shred of evidence that life is serious!" It had a silly looking dog riding in a car with his head out the front window. I started laughing. I loved it! I'm not sure why, but doesn't it seem like as soon as you become an adult, you feel the need to be serious? You start to fill your days with being serious all of the time. Eventually, you've reached middle age, and you evaluate your life and realize that you forgot one of the most important things... to have fun. I've spoken to too many financially successful people who have asked me why it is that even though they have reached their financial goals, they are still not happy. Could it be that they forgot to have fun along the way? I try to infuse fun and laughter into my life every single day. I'm lucky because I have fun people in my life who are good at reminding me to laugh. If you don't have these types of people in your life, try to schedule fun time for yourself every day for 30 days. Have fun every single day for 30 days. Then see how you feel about your life. Life is meant to be enjoyed!

Grow yourself to empower yourself!

Remember: Failure is expected and demanded

of you. If you are not failing, you will not meet success!

Practicing the Art of Imperfect Action:
Questions using Failure to Achieve Success

Fail your way to success, but do it in a smart way. As I have grown as an entrepreneur, I have found there is a formula to transforming a failure to a success. The quicker I'm able to go through this process, the easier it is to reach success. You can also start using this formula in your life to go through the process from failure to success and learning valuable lessons along the way.

5-Step Failure-to-Success Process:

1. **What specifically do I want?** Be clear on what you want. At the beginning of any goal, you must first decide what you want to achieve because clarity is power. Look for what you want and you'll start to see it.

2. **Why is this goal a must?** Why is this goal something I must achieve? Why do I want it so badly that I would do anything to achieve it?

3. **What do I need to do in order to reach my goal?** Take massive imperfect action! In order to reach success, you must work toward your goal. Activity helps you get what you want.

4. **What has worked? What did not work?** Learn from your failures. During the activity, you will need to constantly be evaluating what has worked and what does not work.

5. **Why did it work or not work? What could I change to make it more successful next time?** Change your approach. Whenever you try anything new, you may not be very good at first. You'll need to evaluate what worked and what didn't work to improve. I was just speaking to a friend about failure. He said, "I don't like the word fail. If you learn, how is it a failure?" What an amazing point!

Using the F's where do I need to grow?

As soon as you are able to transform the fear from your life into a meaningful way to grow yourself, you transform your thinking. Your life will truly transform. You change for the better. Your Faith, Family, Friends, Fitness, Finances, Field/Career, or Fun will also change. Little by little, you will be able to use fear to grow yourself.

1. What areas do I need to grow myself in the most right now? (Faith, Family, Friends, Fitness, Finances, Field/Career, or Fun)
2. Choose one or two of the Fs and then pick one specific item you want to work on in each of those areas and focus on growing them.

4

gain
self-confidence

What positive things have you said to yourself today?
Honor your greatness. – Chalene Johnson

Have you ever had one of those days when you
didn't feel very self-confident? I feel like the
universe knew I needed one of those days in order
to effectively write this chapter for you. On this
day a few months back, I did not feel very self-
confident. I was wearing my glasses (if you're
thinking to yourself that wearing glasses isn't so
bad, I wore coke-bottle glasses because my
eyesight was so poor, so yes it was bad. HA!), I

was not feeling well, and I was just turned down for two proposals. Why am I sharing this story? Because I get it. I don't always feel self-confident. I don't always feel like everything will work out. I know how it feels when you don't feel your best. Sometimes you may look at certain people and think they have it all together and that their life is "perfect." What I've learned is that being perfect is definitely an illusion. No one has a perfect life, relationship, children, career, friends, or health.

Recently, I was at a week-long conference. I left my husband in charge of our children and puppy. Each night I'd call home and see how everything was going. He'd say, "I've got this." The night before I returned home, he posted this on social media:

Update on Allison being gone... Day 6. The good: Nobody is missing. The Bad: 2 out of the 4 children sleeping with me last night peed the bed. Logan thought that it would be a good idea to cut his own hair. Juniper the puppy was able to poop in the house three times in less than three hours (that's impressive... I'm not even mad about that). Avery had such a knot in her hair that I had to promise to buy her a toy to comb it out. We have eaten pizza or Subway six nights in a row. Bedtime is usually 8 pm. I actually started the process then, but sadly I fall asleep first so I have no idea what time the children are going to bed. Conclusion: 'I've got this' was a bit of an overstatement. Allison will be home in 24 hours!!!!! We can do it.

That post made me laugh out loud. It's such a great illustration of this point. Have you ever over-projected your self-confidence? I know I have. Then no one helps me out. As soon as my parents saw the post, they immediately called and asked how they could help. If you pretend that you have everything together when you actually don't, it can be draining on you and eventually will hurt the people around you too. Remember that having self-confidence is great. Being overly self-confident in situations when you need help is not okay. You need to recognize the difference, and there is a fine line between the two.

I was just asked this question: "Are you always like this?" I was meeting with a state leader that was interested in growing his leadership skills. I shared some of my journey about increasing my leadership skills. This was the first time I had met him. After speaking to me for about a half an hour, he described me a bit more: "You are so passionate, positive, excited, self-confident, ready to conquer the world, and make an impact. "

Yes, I am.

I don't know what normal is and I don't think I want to be that. – Sharon Ninedorf

For a long time, I thought I was strange because I always had very big visions and a positive outlook on life. I love empowering people to accomplish more in their lives and their business. I've been fortunate to be in many different leadership roles. I've experienced a wide range of people and experiences from an entrepreneur to a non-profit leader.

Do you honor who you are? Have you thought about what strengths and abilities you have? Have you thought about the impact that only you can have? I believe that each of us is on a mission to make an impact in this world. With over seven billion people currently on the planet, we have a lot of different people that can do a lot of different things. The best thing about this is that we all are unique, we all are different, and we all have someone different that we need to help.

Another point to consider when you're dealing

with your self-confidence is that you'll likely never feel self-confident the first time you do anything. I remember leading my first meeting. I had never run a meeting before. I hadn't even created an agenda before. I was nervous that everyone would figure out that I had no clue what I was doing. I had two options. Option one was that I could have gone into the meeting ill-prepared and faked it. Option two was that I could seek help from someone with more experience in that area than me to help me prepare for the meeting. I chose option two. I sat down with a friend and my supervisor and asked them to review the agenda and give me pointers for running an effective meeting. I learned that there are times when you need to recognize that you need to ask for help and learn from others with more experience. When you prepare for the new experience, you gain more self-confidence. There is always someone willing to help. I use this principle in all areas of my life. You should start to think of the areas in your life where you want to grow and then ask yourself, "Who do I know that has done this before and what specific questions would I like answered?"

None of us is as smart as all of us. – Kenneth Blanchard

If self-confidence were an equation, it would look like this:

Opportunity + Action + Risk = Self-Confidence

Successful people use this equation to get results, gain self-confidence, and reach their goals and dreams.

There are times in our lives when we don't act on the things that we know would improve our lives. It goes something like this. You think about an opportunity for a long time, you pass on the opportunity, you over-analyze, then procrastinate, don't take any action, and this all results in you feeling less self-confidence. This is what the equation would look like:

Missed Opportunity + Inaction + No Risk = No Results and Less Self-Confidence

Unfortunately, many people live their entire lives in this equation and they wonder why nothing ever happens to them. They tend to blame others, make excuses, and stay stuck in their lives.

Which equation have you been using? Have you been seeking out opportunities, taking risks, taking action, and then gaining self-confidence? Or have you been missing opportunities, not taking action, not risking anything, and then having no results and less self-confidence?

Perhaps you need to evaluate how you think about this. I want you to take a moment and reflect on your life. Try to think about a time in your life when you had a great opportunity present itself, you took the risk, and took action. How did you feel after that? I bet you felt amazing, self-confident, and successful. What caused this to happen in your life? It was taking the risk and doing something positive.

Now think about the other equation. When in your life did you have an awesome opportunity present itself, but you didn't take the risk and didn't take action? How did you feel afterward? I bet you felt less self-confident.

I think these two equations could possibly transform the next opportunity that comes into your life. I think that you'll see the risk, you'll take action, and then you'll feel self-confident.

However, always remember the opposite is also true.

Steps for Building Your Self-Confidence

I want to share the steps to build self-confidence. By simply changing your perspective, you can change your life.

Step 1: Put your body in motion.

In order to access what's inside of you, it's imperative to move your body through exercise. By moving your body and increasing your heart rate, you'll put yourself into peak state. Professional athletes know this and that is why they push their bodies to do more each and every time they work out. Start with going for a walk every day for 30 days. It's the small changes that will lead to your consistent improvement. Change your body and you'll improve your mind.

For about five years I didn't work out. I purchased food from gas stations or fast food restaurants because I was traveling often. Guess what happened? I gained weight—a lot of weight. I was overweight. It was embarrassing. I felt terrible that I had let it get so bad. I would make a New Year's resolution each year to lose the extra weight, but by February, I would be back to my bad habits. My self-confidence spiraled down. I had negative self-talk at this point in my life. I dreaded getting dressed in the morning because I had to try to find clothes that fit and felt comfortable. Everything was too tight, and some pants I couldn't even pull up. This was frustrating and each day I felt even worse about myself. It's difficult to project your best self when you know that you need to lose weight but haven't yet. It's hard to look in the mirror or even weigh yourself when you know that it will only remind you how you've failed in the area of your health. I started to hate pictures of myself. My husband would tell me I was beautiful, but I wouldn't believe him. I felt terrible about myself. It wasn't fun.

Shortly after my daughter Avery was born, I realized that I had to quit with all of the excuses. I decided to start running. My first run was more of a slow jog/fast walk; it was hard, but I did it. Each day when I would go for a run, I would remind myself that I loved running, that it clears my head, and it feels so good to get healthy. I'd run in the morning, during the day, or at night.

"That day, for no particular reason, I decided to go for a little run. ... I just kept on going.– Forrest Gump

I found that exercising was one of the main things I did to feel more self-confident. It makes me happy to know that I'm healthy on the inside and outside just by exercising. Research shows that exercising releases "feel good" chemicals into our body called endorphins. When we're happy, we have more self-confidence. This translates to us bringing more self-confidence out into the world! Exercise means being physically active in any way you choose. It's really that simple. Just going for a walk, a run, hiking, skiing, or attending an exercise class. Do whatever activity makes you happy. Exercising is a very powerful and easy way that can bring more self-confidence in your life.

Step 2: What is my passion?

Before the age of 18, we hear the word "no" over 100,000 times. This doesn't set us up for success later in our lives. How do you overcome all of those no's? How do you recognize that you are worth it to pursue your passions? Sometimes it's difficult. If you have ever felt that you don't measure up, you need to remind yourself that you are beyond powerful, you are beyond awesome, and you are beyond great.

The self-image is the key to human personality and human behavior. Change the self-image and you change the personality and the behavior. – Maxwell Maltz

Identifying your passion will transform what you focus your energy on. At the end of this chapter, I will share some questions to help you find your passions.

Each of us has all this power inside of us, but you first need to recognize this and focus on getting what you want. For many of us, low self-confidence stems from our inner self-talk that we've been conditioned to do for years. Unfortunately, many of us, without even realizing it, criticize ourselves. The great thing is that it only takes making a decision to make a change to alter the trajectory of your life. Today you can make the decision to make the change.

As you start off on your path, you'll inevitably be met with obstacles. Why is this so difficult, you'll wonder? I'm going to be painfully honest here. For a long time, I felt like I did not have anything to offer the world. I undervalued my time. I gave everything away for free. I settled for much less than what I was worth. I did this because deep down I had given myself excuses for why I did not have any worth. I blamed my family, my upbringing, where I lived, my education, and more. All of the stories I'd been telling myself for years, the stories that made myself feel less than enough, were false, but they kept me comfortable. Then one day I was listening to my mentor, Oprah (okay, so she's my mentor from afar... but someday I will meet her and share with her all of the useful lessons she has given me). She was talking about the limiting stories that hold us back from our greatness. She shared about how she had interviewed over 35,000 people and that after the camera went off, each of them asked her, "Did I do okay?" They wanted to be validated (Winfrey, 2013). They wanted to make sure their worth was there, that their voice was heard, and that they did well. Just hearing her describe that made me feel better. If presidents and famous people sometimes felt less than adequate, then it was okay for me to feel that way too.

Write down your passion and focus on it.

Step 3: Decide and commit.

The next step is to decide on and commit to your goal or passion. I was just talking to a friend about her son. She said her son wants to try something new and she told him, "Take the risk; what's the worst thing that could happen?" What amazing advice! We all need someone to say, "Take the risk! Make the decision and do it!" I'm going to let you in on a little secret. You'll always be afraid the first time you try something—always. You gain self-confidence after you take action and do it. It's the action that builds your self-confidence.

By deciding to do something, you'll set yourself up for success. Even if you don't know "how" to reach your goal, you'll start to figure out the resources you need to reach the goal.

I had a friend that set a goal for her business. She is a photographer and was just starting off. She decided to book ten senior sessions in one summer. This was a crazy huge goal for her because she had never done it. I remember the day she told me about this goal. It was that day that she set herself up for success. Her process was first to decide on the goal she wanted to achieve. Then she decided to write down the goal. After that she let me know that she was going after this goal and asked for my support. A few short months later she let me know that she booked all ten sessions. She was ecstatic. The great thing about this process is that as soon as you decide on your goal and commit to it, you are setting yourself up for success in reaching your goal.

Step 4: Take action to serve others.

My Great-Aunt Margaret taught me that "life is too short to sit around thinking about yourself all day." She has lived her life by the service motto. You would not meet a happier, kinder, and more compassionate person. When I spent time with Great-Aunt Margaret, I was amazed by her service to others. She regularly took action to serve others in her family, church, and community. She was intentional about finding a way to help someone else every single day. What did serving others do for Great-Aunt Margaret? It helped her to stop thinking so much about herself.

Sometimes in our lives, we get obsessed with ourselves and all of our problems. We go over and over things in our heads, worry, feel anxious and then feel less than enough. Guess what doing all of these things lead to? It leads to low self-confidence. Have you ever heard that if you want to become a millionaire, all you need to do is help one million people get what they want?

Whenever you're thinking too much about yourself, you will notice that your life becomes dull. People don't want to be around people that think about themselves all the time. Here is a simple question to ask yourself each and every day: How can I serve someone today? One of the things that I missed for a long time in my life was service because I told myself I was so busy. If you own a business or you work in any organization, you are in the service business. Busyness is just an excuse. We are all busy. Each of us has seven days a week and 24 hours each day. When I was not being intentional about how I was going to serve others, my results showed. I lacked self-confidence, and I wasn't achieving the results that I wanted. When I started to intentionally think about what I could do to help others, I had magnificent results in my personal and professional life. I ask myself, "How am I serving others?" and "What am I going to do today in order to add value to somebody's life?" The main reason that we are here is to help others. If we want to lead a bigger life and have a bigger impact, then we simply need to help more people.

It's similar to when your child is sick and you're taking care of them. You are putting 100% into making sure your sick child feels more comfortable so their tiny body can heal as soon as possible. You show them love, take them to the doctor, give them medicine, and turn on their favorite cartoon. By the end of the day, how are you feeling? I bet you feel love because you just spent the entire day with all of your energy focused on someone else. Focusing your energy on someone else causes magical things to happen to us. It's like as soon as we give up control and focus more on others, we can connect with our higher self. We connect with a different part of ourselves. We connect with our divine source and the universal force that wants good things to happen. Once you're in that place, you will then want to continue your focus on others and make more of a significant impact. You'll find that as soon as you do, the world will open up to you.

Step 5: Believe there is good in the world! Be the good.

I have a sign in my office that says, "Believe

there is good in the world! Be the Good." Be that person that goes above and beyond what people need and become EXTRAordinary. You need to understand where you are and where you are going, but along the way you need to become the best version of yourself. Be the first person to congratulate someone else. Be that person that other people want to be around. Be that person that takes care of others. Be the person who loves on others. Be the person who wants the best for others. Be that awesome person that you are, and you will gain self-confidence. People will recognize that about you. Many times, we get stomped down by the negativity that comes into our lives. What if, rather than focusing on all that negativity, we focused on the positive? Have you ever heard that life will pay whatever price you ask it?

Step 6: Dress for success.

This step is about how you project yourself to the world externally. How many of you have put on sweatpants and a sweatshirt and hung out on the couch all day eating chips and watching Netflix? I'm sure many of us have had those days. It may feel comfortable, but I bet your self-confidence level is fairly low. Now imagine that you want to have a very self-confident day. You want to be filled with self-confidence. Do you wear sweatpants and a sweatshirt to that important meeting? NO! My husband is a great example of how dressing for success can make a difference. For many years he wore khakis and a polo shirt to work. Then one day he decided to wear a dress shirt with a tie and dress pants. By changing what he was wearing, he felt more self-confident. And guess what happened to the sales at our business? They grew dramatically. This is a simple way to build your confidence.

When you're thinking about how you are projecting yourself out into this world, you need to be cautious of what you're wearing. I keynote speak and conduct leadership trainings at large conventions. I'm intentional about what I wear at these events. I choose outfits that I know will stand out because I want to look differently than the rest of the people at the event. I want to stand out. You need to be aware of what you look like. Too many people do not take the time and effort to really think about what they look like and how their clothes reflect their level of success. It is critical for us to be very well groomed if we want to have that next position or gain the new clients for our business. Dressing for success will give you self-confidence. This is critical to your success.

If you are not comfortable doing this, find a friend or a stylist to help you figure it out. Schedule a makeover day for yourself. Men can and should do this too. I've brought my husband to the store to buy a new outfit. Find a friend to come to the store with you to help make sure the outfit fits well on you. Schedule a hair appointment at a nice salon and then go do some clothes shopping. There are so many affordable resources online that can help you look your best. If you look your best, you will project your best into the world. Look for the one great outfit that makes you feel really awesome. Then go out to dinner with friends or your spouse. I'm pretty sure you will be feeling like a million bucks!

Start thinking about what makes you the best version of you. It's not just about vanity. Decide today that you're going to start bringing your best self into this world. When you dress really well, have your hair done, and feel self-confident, guess what that shows people? They recognize that you are bringing your best self to the world. People will start to treat you a lot differently... in a good way. Put your best version into the world!

Step 7: Put yourself out there.

Another fear that I had when I decided to write my first book was putting myself out there. Did you know that most people are more afraid of success than they are of failing? Putting yourself out there can be a scary thing. Having everyone know who you are can be unnerving. I can be reserved and private, and I wondered if I wrote a book and put myself out there what would happen? How would I get treated? What would I do if people were negative toward me? I really struggled with this for a long time. I remember telling my husband about it and he said the exact words I needed to hear: "What if it's better than you could have imagined? What if you help people design lives they love? What then?"

As I changed my perspective, I could see that I needed to follow my dream of writing a book. I wasn't going to help anyone if I kept everything to myself. I had unique experiences, mentors, thoughts, and ideas that needed to be shared. After this realization, I went out on a mission to help ONE person with my book. I wrote and edited the book in the hopes that one person would be positively impacted by my book, *Life Under Construction: Designing a Life You Love.* I truly believe that to give is to live. Whenever I'm feeling insecure about putting myself out there, I remind myself, "What if I am able to help one person?" Even now, when I'm standing on stage speaking to hundreds and even thousands of people, I tell myself that there is one person out there that needs my message today. One person. Just one person. I'm doing it for that one person because when I focus on helping them, guess what automatically happens? I forget about all of my reasons and excuses for why I can't do it. When I focus on others, I go all in. I take all of the energy, and I use it for good.

Step 8: Focus on being more self-confident.

If you want to have the self-confidence, you need to start to act like you are self-confident before you really feel self-confident. I know that sounds a little weird, but it's true. You need to tell yourself that you are self-confident. You have the choice to choose high-energy, positive emotions: love, happiness, joy, laughter, excitement, awe, contentment, passion, and enthusiasm. Or you can focus on low-energy, negative emotions: anger, greed, jealousy, stress, fear, not enough, scared, worry, anxiety, and guilt. In the book *Psycho-Cybernetics*, Maxwell Maltz explains, "Your self-image must be a reasonable approximation of 'you' being neither more than you are nor less than you are. When this self-image is intact and secure, you feel secure, you feel good. When it is threatened, you feel anxious and insecure. When your self-image is adequate and one that you can be proud of, you feel self-confident. You feel free to 'be yourself' and to express yourself."

I'm a fairly happy and enthusiastic person, but there are times in my life when I did not feel this way. Have you heard where your focus goes, energy flows? Think about it in your life. In a typical week, do you focus more on what's missing from your life or what's in your life? Recently, I was at a conference learning from Tony Robbins and he asked people to write down all of the emotions they felt each week. He said that most of us only feel 12 or so emotions. Of those, about six of them are negative and six are positive. He said that many times people automatically feel the same emotions over and over again. If you tend to be an angry person, you're probably going to feel angry a lot, which subsequently will lead to you feeling low energy and less confidence. Do you focus more on what's out of your control or what's in your control? If you tend to focus on things that are out of your control, you may feel more anxious, worried, and upset. This is also a low-energy state. Do you focus more on the past, present, or the future? If you focus on either the past or the future too much, it can cause you to be less content in your life because you're living your life in a place beyond your control. Being present or mindful is a key part of your contentment and fulfillment in life. Also, if you focus on what's missing from your life or what you can't control, or something that happened in the past, you'll likely feel depressed. By simply focusing on different answers to these questions, you can dramatically change how you feel about your life. Live it!

Step 9: Tell yourself: Actually, I can!

To each, there comes in their lifetime a special moment when they are figuratively tapped on the shoulder and offered the chance to do a very special thing, unique to them and fitted to their talents. What a tragedy if that moment finds them unprepared or unqualified for that which could have been their finest hour. – Winston Churchill

Right now, you are being figuratively tapped on the shoulder, and it's your time. We need you to step into your greatness—right now. We need you to take action on that dream you've held within you for so long.

Many people take their passions and dreams for granted. Do you know why this is? Because for their entire lives they have been diminished by the people who loved them the most. Did you know your close family and friends are often times your worst critics? Do you know why that is? It's because when you begin to share with others your dream of a bigger life and having a more significant impact, those people automatically look at their lives and think to themselves, "Well, I can't go after my dreams and goals." They falsely assume that because they haven't or can't, neither can you. You are a threat to their comfortable life. You are a threat to their excuses for not stepping into their greatness. You are the very thing that scares them the most because you are willing to push forward to chase your dreams and goals.

That, my friends, makes people quite uncomfortable.

I remember a specific time I had to deal with this. I was enjoying a holiday dinner with family when one family member said to me, "So how's that speaking thing coming? Whatcha doing?" At the time, I had just decided to start pursuing my passion for writing, speaking, training, and coaching. I've been speaking since I was in third grade, and I have won awards for my speaking, so I knew that I could be good at it. But at the time, I was still uncomfortable with the newness of chasing my dreams. I replied, "It's going fabulously. Thanks for asking." That's it. So, if you get a similar question (and believe me you will), all you need to say is, "It's going great!" or "Wow, I'm so excited about it!" And if you want to be a little nosey, ask that person, "Do you have a big goal you're chasing? How's that going for you?" At least 99% of the time, that person has a goal or dream that they are too afraid to chase, and now that you're going for your dream, it is making them very uncomfortable. Your imperfect action is ruining the excuses they've created for themselves.

Okay, so now do you believe me? Do you realize

that you are the exact person that needs to chase that goal? It's YOU! If you don't do it, NO ONE ELSE WILL! Seriously! You are the exact right person to chase that crazy huge dream you have. You are the one to do it. There is a reason that you were gifted with that idea. Have you ever thought about your ideas as gifts? They are gifts. They are precious gifts, and they are more precious than gold because ideas can change the world!

All of us want more self-confidence. The sooner you realize you are really worth the effort, the more quickly you'll gain self-confidence. You need to put your best face on, dress for success, bring your best version to the world, exercise daily, and serve others. Believe there is good in the world! Be the good! Put yourself out there and tell yourself, "Actually, I can!"

Remember: You've got this!

Practicing the Art of Imperfect Action: Questions to Gain Self-Confidence

Did you know that you have the option to choose how you will act and perceive yourself?

Close your eyes and imagine your best day ever. Today you get to do that thing you are so passionate about doing. You feel self-confident and strong. You're happy because you get to serve all of those people that you love to serve. Your hair is done and you're wearing a new outfit. You feel like a million bucks. Now open your eyes. I want you to write down the words that describe you in the best version of yourself.

1. How do you feel?
2. Who are you serving?
3. Where are you?
4. What are you doing?
5. Why does this make you feel excited?
6. What are the things in your life that make you happy?
7. What do you love?
8. What do you despise?
9. What are you passionate about?
10. What do you really want?

I'd encourage you to write down the words that you feel describe yourself. Write down everything that comes to mind. Don't judge the words that you wrote down, just leave them for a day. The next day, look at the words and put a (+) or a (-) by each word to indicate whether it is a positive or negative way to see yourself. Do you have more positives or more negatives? If you have more negatives, I want you to write down the best words you can say about yourself. If you're having a difficult time seeing the good in yourself, ask someone who loves you to share some positive words that describe you.

Congratulations! You now have a new picture of who you are. You are this positive version of yourself. Now I want you to read those positive words to yourself every day for 21 days. Before you read each word, say, "I am." This one exercise will dramatically transform your life.

5

jump—don't step—out of your comfort zone!

What are you afraid of? How does it make you feel? Instead of letting your fear get the best of you, find out how to fully experience it, name it, get to know it and take it by the hand so it can become your friend and ally. Bless you, for your fear for it is a sign of wisdom. Do not hold yourself in fear. Transform the energy to flexibility and you will be free from what you fear. – Yoko Ono

How many of you are afraid to do something right now? I bet every single one of you shook your head, "YES, ME!" It doesn't matter where you live or what language you speak. I've spoken with people from all over the world and I've heard it over and over again. People say to me, "I'm afraid to _____." We're all afraid of something. I was recently doing a training for entrepreneurs in Nigeria. At the end of the presentation, I had time for questions. During that time, I had multiple people ask me, "What do you do when you feel afraid?" I was also recently at an event in the United States and got asked the exact same question: "What do I do when I feel fear?"

The first thing I want to say about fear is that it is good... in a way. Fear is something the brain uses to protect us. Back in the days of hunters and gatherers, we used fear to protect ourselves from being attacked by lions and tigers and bears... oh my. Fear was a pretty useful tool in those circumstances. However, as we have evolved as a species, we are still feeling fear, even though there are no lions, tigers, or bears literally chasing us—at least I hope not. We have fear flood into our bodies when we send in a resume for a new job or a proposal to a new client, or when we pick up the phone to call that person, or send the email, or have the tough conversation.

There is also emotional fear that you feel if you have something terrible happening. For example, if you read my first book, *Life Under Construction: Designing a Life You Love,* you heard about my airplane trip. During that airplane trip, I felt emotional fear because the plane was going down. That is a real fear. I'm not referring to this fear when I talk about stepping outside of your comfort zone.

Overcoming F.E.A.R.: False Evidence Appearing Real (Shapiro, 2010)

Everyone knows fear. It can come in an instant and throw you into chaos, yet it can also save your life. Fear is a natural response to physical danger, but it can also be self-created, such as the fear of failure, being out of control, being different, or being lonely. There is a fear of the future and of death. You may fear love because you fear being rejected; fear being generous because you fear you will not have enough; fear sharing your thoughts or feelings in case you appear wrong, and fear trusting because you are dominated by self-doubt and insecurity.

This self-generated fear is found in its acronym: F.E.A.R. or False Evidence Appearing Real. It appears real, even though it is a fear of the future and is not happening now. Therefore, it has no real substance, arising when the ego-self is threatened, which makes you cling to the known and familiar. Such fear creates untold worry, apprehension, nervous disorders, and even paranoia.

If fear is just false evidence appearing real, then you don't really have to worry about anything, do you? I understand that for most of you, fear feels very real. It doesn't feel false at all.

I have a picture that shows the difference between life inside and outside the comfort zone. On the right side, there is a circle labeled as "your comfort zone." On the other side of the page, there's a big circle that says "where the magic happens." When we are in our comfort zone, our brain is happy. It likes when we do the same things, talk to the same people, and live in our routines. However, everything exciting that we want in life lives outside of our comfort zone. That can be SCARY! How in the world are we supposed to reach our goals and dreams when we're afraid? How are we supposed to start that new business? Go back to school? Start that new relationship? How? I remember seeing this illustration and thinking how brilliant it is. This is so helpful because so many of us love to stay in our comfort zone.

Fear can hold us back. I know that in my own

life when I am going to start a new project or goal, I may feel afraid and fearful at the start. I was recently working on hosting my first *Life Under Construction Live Event*. I've had people asking me to do a full-day training event. I've hosted many trainings and was excited thinking about the event. But after I found a location and started to work on a date and the details of the event, fear started to flood into my brain. *What if no one comes? How am I going to do everything? I don't have enough time. I'm going to need help.* I wondered why I was feeling so afraid, but then I recognized that it was because I was stepping outside of my comfort zone. I assured myself that I was prepared for this, and I already had everything I needed in order to succeed. What I recognized is that our brains like to keep us safe, they want to help us survive. However, when we begin to do different things in our lives, we start stepping outside our comfort zone and that is when fear floods in.

Life begins at the end of your comfort zone. – Neil Donald Walsh

Well, guess what? That's where the magic happens! Outside your comfort zone is where the magic lives, but as soon as we step out is when we start to feel fear. To help myself remember to continually step out of my comfort zone, I got a bracelet that says "fearless." I wanted to remind myself that I can start being fearless, and I don't need to feel that fear when I'm trying to get to the magic to reach all of my goals and dreams. Realizing this was a big turning point in my life. I'm continually pushing myself outside of my comfort zone. I'm going to have bigger results and I'm going to have more awesome things happening in my life. I'm going to start implementing the art of imperfect action.

How to JUMP outside your comfort zone:

1. **Decide.** Make the decision that you want MORE. You want MORE in your life, career, personal life, and relationships. This takes making the decision to do the very things that make you afraid.

2. **Ask yourself, "What am I most afraid to do right now?"** What is the one thing you are most afraid of right now? I've found the thing I'm most afraid to do right now is probably the next thing I need to do. It's the fear that tells us that we will be stepping outside of our comfort zone. Finishing this book and sharing it with

the world is my next scary goal. I've already written a book, but I'm stepping outside of my comfort zone again. I'm putting my ideas, stories, and thoughts out there for people all over the world to read. It also makes me want to jump in the air with excitement at the same time. I get jazzed up thinking about the impact this book will have on people's lives. My purpose is to empower you to be, do, and design a life you love. I think this book will help you understand why you may be feeling stuck and how you can move forward by practicing the art of imperfect action.

3. **When fear floods in, tell yourself, "I'm just stepping outside of my comfort zone."** You're ready; you've committed yourself to face your fears. You've identified the one thing that you are the most afraid of right now. You're taking those first steps to face your fear. And it feels like you are walking through mud. Really! You're just trudging through the mud and it feels like you're sinking because each step you take is harder and

harder. You may be thinking to yourself, "Allison, I thought I was supposed to do this so I could get to where the magic happens." And you are. However, the kicker is that it takes walking in the mud for a while before you start to get any results. Don't give up. If you study any successful person, you'll read about how many times they had to fail before they succeeded. As my daughter Avery says, "Put your muddy puddle boots on and get going!" You're on your way now. There's no turning back. You don't want to always wonder what could have been.

Remember, the magic happens outside your comfort zone. All of your hopes and dreams and magic lives outside your comfort zone. If you want to stay stuck in your comfort zone doing the same things, talking to the same people, and hoping that it's going to just change, you're going to be disappointed. Unfortunately, most people are forced out of their comfort zone because something life-changing happens to them: they lose a job, lose a loved one, move, start or end a relationship, have a major health scare, or start a family.

If you want to take charge of your life, it's important to constantly be stepping outside of your comfort zone. Every day do something uncomfortable. For myself, I started by sharing more on social media, writing, and speaking. I would share what I was learning and what I was doing. Typically, I'm pretty reserved, so sharing what I was doing freaked me out at first. I thought it was kind of strange to do that. Then one day I received a Facebook message from a college friend of mine. She said, "Hi Allison! Not sure if you remember me from Tech, but I've been watching you via Facebook and I just wanted to tell you how proud I am of you. Maybe that's weird coming from a kind of stranger. But wow, you're really doing life the way I hope to someday." I was humbled by this message because I feel like I was just being me. I was trying to make a positive impact in some small way. Who is out there that needs you to start being you? To share your strengths with the world? I know what you're thinking right now: "Allison, I don't have anything special to share." YOU DO! Each of the seven billion people on this earth is unique and we're gifted with talents. We need you to be the best version of yourself.

Are you ready to JUMP out of your comfort zone? Are you ready to face your fears? Are you ready to get your muddy puddle boots on and start failing forward? I hope so! We desperately need you to start. There is so much potential inside of you that isn't being tapped. Yet.

Remember: You have greatness within you that could change someone's life.

Practicing the Art of Imperfect Action: Questions to Help You Jump Outside of Your Comfort Zone!

1. How has fear held you back from attempting new things in your life?
2. Do you want MORE in your life? If so, what does that look like for you?
3. What are you most afraid to do right now? (Hint: this may be the next thing you need to do.)
4. Write down everything you do each day. Then write down everything you do each week. Then write down everything you do each month. Are you doing the same

things over and over again? If so, think of
ways to try new things.

6

set crazy huge goals

Set goals that match your potential, not your ability. – Grant Cardone

Definition of Goal: Something that you are trying to do or achieve. (Merriam Webster , 2018)

Do you want to achieve massive results in your life? Did you know the time to act on ideas is immediately? Think about it. How many times in your life have you forgotten an awesome idea because you didn't take any action or even write it down?

Today I'm going to teach you the secrets that super-successful people use when setting and achieving CRAZY huge goals in their lives. These are secrets that I've learned through mentorship with successful people and researching multi-millionaires and billionaires. The information I'm sharing I didn't just "make up." I've implemented these secrets in my life and I've experienced results. These are the secrets for creating massive success in your life.

Did you know that most people are scared of success? That is the exact reason for most people settling in their lives. They settle in their lives because they are scared of success. They've said that money is evil or that money changes people for their entire lives.

Our deepest fear is not that we are inadequate. Our deepest fear is that we are powerful beyond measure. It is our light, not our darkness, that most frightens us. – Marianne Williamson

I have one mentor who says, "The world needs you rich." At first, I was very uncomfortable with him saying this to me. "I don't want to be greedy," I thought. Then I thought a bit more about it, and I realized that he's right both in terms of money and service toward others. The world needs us rich. Do you know why I say that? I know the type of person that picks up my book:

You are interested in personal development and you are passionate about helping others.

Think about it. What would you do with $46 billion? Well, one of the richest couples in the United States, Melinda and Bill Gates, have given billions of dollars to charity (Gates Foundation, 2017). Warren Buffett plans on giving away 99% of his money and is currently accepting letters to decide who will receive that money (Buffet, 2010). Can you imagine having that much money? How many mouths could you feed with $46 billion? How many children could you educate or provide health care for? How many businesses could you fund? How many schools could you build? And this is probably one of my favorite questions: How many countries could you transform?

Really think about it. A friend recently asked me this question as we were driving by a mansion: "Allison, what would you do with an extra $10 million?" I had a list of ideas, but one of my favorites was to have a school built in Paraguay—and I already know where the school will be built. I recently traveled to Paraguay with John C. Maxwell and his team to conduct trainings on values-based transformational leadership. It was one of the most amazing experiences in my life. During the week-long trainings, our team of 100 coaches trained over 15,000 people, which, at the time of writing this book, has resulted in over 120,000 people receiving training in that country. There was one particular training that I missed being a part of because I had to catch my flight home. The team visited students at a school located next to a landfill in Asuncion, Paraguay. Do you know what the students do with items from the landfill? They recycle these items into musical instruments and learn to play beautiful music. Orchestra director Favio Chavez describes what they are doing: "The world sends us garbage... we send back music." They are named the Recycled Orchestra of Cateura (www.landfillharmonicmovie.com).

These amazing students are traveling all over the world to perform with their recycled instruments and have been featured on world news and media. I have seen pictures of their school, and I'd love to help them rebuild or expand it. That's a crazy huge goal!

Let me share something with you about setting crazy huge goals. You will know that you've set a crazy huge goal when you're a bit afraid of it. A crazy huge goal should NEVER feel comfortable. If you are not afraid of your goal, then you are setting it too small. You need to get comfortable with being uncomfortable if you're going to start setting CRAZY huge goals.

I recently asked my friend Timothy Teasdale to share his perspective on success. Timothy Teasdale and his wife Gaby lead the Transformacion Paraguay office in Paraguay to bring transformational leadership to that country. I met Timothy and Gaby while I was in Paraguay as a transformational leadership coach in that country. I was inspired by Timothy and Gaby's passion to transform their country. Their professionalism, commitment, and kindness were demonstrated in everything they did. I've asked Timothy to share his perspective on what success looks like when trying to transform a country.

What Does Success Mean in Transforming a Country?

By Timothy Teasdale, Director, Transformacion Paraguay, www.transformacion.org

Success to me means doing something that is worthwhile. In this century, we are living an instant life, everything comes fast and easy. Too often it seems as though we have forgotten about the values of hard work and determination. As one of the leaders of Transformacion Paraguay, I can tell you that it was a lot of hard work and determination to bring a transformational movement to the country of Paraguay, but it was all worthwhile. People told us 'no' more times than I can count. Friends literally told us that they do not believe in us and our vision. But, when you recognize how people's lives are being transformed through the lessons they are learning in the Roundtable, it was all worthwhile.

Find something that you are willing to bleed for, sweat for, work your butt off for, cry for, and even die for—that is something worthwhile. When you can work on that thing, your purpose, your mission, your passion, each and every day, even in the face of adversity and failure, that is my definition of success. At the end of life, you will be able to say it was all worth it, the time I spent on this planet, I made a difference, I left a mark, I made a difference, it was all worthwhile.

About Transformacion Paraguay from their website www.transformacion.org: In partnership with The John Maxwell Leadership Foundation (the Foundation Leadership John Maxwell), Paraguay offers lessons in Transformation Roundtable Leadership at no cost to thousands of organizations and hundreds of thousands of people. All leadership lessons were designed after extensive research in Paraguay and developed in collaboration with Dr. John C. Maxwell, the world's number one leadership expert.

Our goal is to train 10% of the Paraguayan population in leadership values. Research has suggested that if a country can bring a positive change to 10% of its people, this 10% will then have a multiplier effect that will reach the entire population. Examples of this include The Civil Rights Movement in the United States in the '50s and '60s and the Anti-Apartheid Movement in South Africa.

Each time I read Timothy's description of success, it brings tears to my eyes—and I feel inspired. Timothy and Gaby have so much love and passion for their country of Paraguay. They believe in their goal of transforming their country.

Why did I share this with you? Because I want you to stretch yourself. We need you to step up into your greatness. Just like Gaby and Timothy Teasdale, we need more people who are willing to become so passionate and committed to their goals that they would do almost anything to see them become a reality. The vision of transforming an entire country can be very daunting. Can you even imagine feeling like this is what you're called to do? After meeting them and seeing their passion for completing their goal, I have no doubt that they will reach their goal of transforming their country. Through this work, they will also inspire people in other countries around the world to do the same! WOW! I love this.

I wrote about five mistakes in goal setting in my book *Life Under Construction: Designing a Life You Love*. I want to review them here for you because I know they will help you. When I find information that will help you, it's worth repeating.

As you design your life, you must craft your goals carefully. Another of my mentors, Paul Martinelli, President of the John Maxwell Team, has taught me some of the most common mistakes we can make when setting up our goals. In his presentation *The 5 Mistakes of Goal Setting*, Paul defines the five biggest goal-setting mistakes as setting goals we know we can achieve; setting goals based on fixed plans; believing a goal isn't "real" if we don't know exactly how to achieve it; questioning the right to "do," "be," or "have" what we want; and thinking that a goal's true purpose is reaching the goal itself. He has given me permission to share these mistakes with you.

Mistake 1: Setting goals we know we can achieve.

When setting goals, sometimes you might think, "I'm pretty sure that I could do this because I did something similar last year." This isn't setting a true goal; it's using what you already know you can accomplish as a baseline for future achievement. The problem with this type of thinking is that it limits your ability to push yourself out of your comfort zone. Goals are meant to be big—so big that when you achieve a goal, you stop and think, "Wow, I did that." Don't limit yourself by comparing your potential accomplishments to what you've done in the past. It won't work and it will limit you.

Instead, you should choose goals that are not attainable in your mind right now but would be absolutely amazing to achieve. Think of something that you've always wanted to do, but that your negative voice said you couldn't. Now ignore that voice and write the goal down. It's that simple.

Mistake 2: Setting goals based on a fixed plan.

In my previous job, we had to create strategic plans for everything. Our goals not only had to be tangibly measurable but also had to fit inside preexisting plans. We might have had a wonderful and amazing idea for a goal, but if the idea didn't fit into the original plan, it got thrown out. I bet we lost many great ideas and goals just because they didn't fit into the current plan. What a shame!

Don't worry about preset plans when setting your goals. If a great goal pops into your head but it doesn't fit your current plans, write it down anyway. Allow for the possibility to arise when setting goals.

Mistake 3: Believing a goal isn't "real" if we don't know exactly how to achieve it.

It would be nice if all our goals came with a roadmap. It's common to want absolute clarity about how to achieve a goal before attempting it. But goals don't work like this. In fact, not being sure of how to reach your goal is sometimes an important part of the achievement process. In order for you to become more than you are right now, you need to choose goals that push you outside of your comfort zone. That means that you won't be 100% comfortable with your goal and you'll be working outside of your area of expertise. That's okay. You don't need to know how to accomplish something for it to be a goal—you'll figure it out along the way.

Mistake 4: Questioning the right to "do," "be," or "have" what we want.

As you start setting goals, you may start thinking to yourself, "I don't deserve that," or "I'm just not..." or "I can't..." If you find yourself thinking negative thoughts like these, *stop it*! This is self-sabotage. We are all human beings: there is no such thing as "less than" someone else, and no one inherently "deserves" any more than you do. If you want something, go for it. Why couldn't you be, have, or become exactly who or what you want? Don't let your negative voices creep into your head. Your life should be amazing, and there is enough for everyone. You don't need to compare yourself to anyone else. This is your life. You are designing it the exact way that you want it to turn out. Set your goal and tell yourself, "Yes, I deserve this. I can make my life exactly what I want it to be."

Mistake 5: Thinking the purpose of a goal is reaching the goal itself.

This is my favorite myth. Goals are important, yes, but achieving them isn't the true purpose behind them. Achieving goals takes preparation, time, and effort—a real investment of many different resources. Yet, when you reach your goal, you'll realize that something greater has been happening all along, something behind the scenes. While you were sacrificing your time and energy, this *thing* happened inside of you and it transformed you. You became the person who just achieved the goal.

The purpose of a goal isn't merely to reach the goal—it's much more than that. The purpose is to become someone who can *achieve*. To achieve your goal, you had to grow and change: this is a goal's true purpose.

You must commit to becoming a goal-setting pro in order to design a life you will love. Setting goals is a critical part of your successful journey because goals help us pinpoint specific things we want or need in our lives. As Norman Vincent Peale, author of *The Power of Positive Thinking*, once said, "All successful people have a goal. No one can get anywhere unless he knows where he wants to go and what he wants to be or do."

You've Set a CRAZY Huge Goal! NOW WHAT?

1. **When you see it, you MUST ACT.** Ideas have a short shelf life. That crazy huge goal that you just wrote down needs to be acted on RIGHT NOW! You need to take some small action toward that goal immediately so that your brain establishes that this goal is important to you. Every idea has energy. If you increase the energy of an idea by taking massive action, that anchors the idea and belief. However, the opposite is true as well. If you don't take action, then guess what happens to the idea or goal? It diminishes. Take imperfect action toward your goal.

2. **Trust you are the right person to chase the crazy huge goal.** After you set a CRAZY huge goal, you'll almost immediately think to yourself, "I've never done anything like this in my life and

I'm terrified," or "I've never met anyone that has done anything like this," or "WHAT AM I THINKING?" or "Who am I to do this crazy huge thing?" and on and on and on. Congratulations! You've officially chosen a goal that is located outside of your comfort zone! Celebrate this uncomfortable feeling because it means you are growing. It also means you're about to have a lot of AWESOME things come into your life. Trust you are the right person to chase this crazy huge goal.

3. **Stop and listen to your intuition.** Now what I'd like you to do is sit in a quiet place away from distractions and get really quiet. Take a deep breath. Be present. If you'd like, you can play some soft, relaxing music. I want you to take a moment to connect to your heart. I'd like you to connect with that inner guiding voice. Listen for it. Do you hear it? If not, take a moment to breathe. As you hear it guiding you, take note of what it's telling you. Make no judgment about what it is telling you. Simply note the message and then go back to breathing. Try this practice every day for at least 5-10 minutes. Eventually, increase the time that you sit to listen to your intuition. This is one of

the most powerful ways that you will move forward.

4. **Get laser focused.** If you want to be successful in achieving your goal, you need to devote your time and energy to accomplish that goal with laser focus. I'd like you to get laser-focused on one crazy huge goal. I'd encourage you to write it down on post-it notes and hang them up around the house and in your office. Everywhere you look you should be able to see your crazy huge goal. By doing this, you are reminding yourself to be laser-focused on taking action on that goal every single day. You need to be very laser-focused on your goal if you want to achieve it. Think about how a laser condenses a beam of light. It focuses in on one specific area in order to be effective. A laser does not spread its light everywhere. Remember to be laser-focused on this goal!

5. **Stop Worrying About What Others Will Think!**
You probably wouldn't worry about what people think of you if you could know how seldom they do! – Olin Miller
This was one of my biggest obstacles in

overcoming my perfectionism. I continually worried about what others would think if I did the thing I wanted to do next. What if I wrote a book? What would people think? What if I started to chase my crazy huge goal? What would people think? When I saw that quote above, I realized that I didn't have to worry about what others were thinking about me because they probably weren't! HA! This was such a freeing concept for me. People are not worried about me, so why should I be worried about what they might think about what I am doing? I shouldn't! I decided to stop caring about what others might think about my crazy huge goals. I realized that I needed to live my life for my purpose. For the majority of my life, I had been letting my concern about what others might think to keep me from taking action on my goals. While I am upset that I let this false story have power over me, I realize that I needed to learn that lesson in order to teach it to you. Please take my advice and don't worry about what others might think, because most likely they don't care as much as you think. Only the people who truly care for you want the best for you.

Remember: Believe in yourself. If you don't, then who will?

Practicing the Art of Imperfect Action:
Questions to Help You Set CRAZY Huge
Goals

1. What is the biggest goal you have ever set
   for yourself? Did you reach it? How did it
   feel if you did?
2. What is the next goal you want to set for
   yourself?
3. Why is this goal important to you?
4. What will you achieve after you reach the
   goal?
5. How will you know that you achieved the
   goal?
6. What resources do you need to achieve
   the goal?
7. How much time will you need to reach
   the goal?
8. When would you like to achieve the goal
   by?
9. What other ideas do you have that will
   help you be successful to reach your goal?

7

finding your inner magic

As you think, so shall you become. – Bruce Lee

I never realized how much I distrusted myself until I was faced with the task of stepping into my purpose. I realized as I started to work on myself more and more that for years I really struggled with feeling that I wasn't enough. I did not trust my innate abilities and inner magic to do, be, or have what I wanted in my life. How many of us do this type of self-sabotage constantly? By not trusting myself, I was allowing myself to stay in a place where I felt stuck. I constantly sought answers, but deep down I was unsettled with myself. I was unhappy with myself, and I did not trust that I could be the person I wanted to become. I could not help the people that I wanted to help. I gave myself excuses about my family, environment, education, and appearance, and they were all the reasons I didn't trust myself.

At one of the lowest points in my life, I found trust in myself. I found that I had everything I needed already within me. The power was already within me, and all I needed to do was access it. That day a shift occurred because I had accessed my inner magic. I stopped the excuses. I harnessed trust. I believed that I could. Each of us is gifted with truly amazing dreams. We think that these are just fake dreams, but in reality, these are specifically chosen for us. I truly believe that within each of us are the seeds of greatness. As we learn to trust ourselves and the infinite power within us, we are able to become more than we could have imagined. Trusting your power will transform your life.

For as long as I can remember, I've been on a quest to find my inner magic. I've been consumed with figuring out what makes me me. Why am I like this? I remember reading for hours and hours as a child and being transported into someone else's life. I remember comparing that person with me and thinking, Why am I like this? Have you ever asked yourself this question?

Well, I figured out the secret. I'm like this because this is who I am. I'm a little outgoing, friendly, stubborn, determined, and analytical because that is who I am meant to be. As a child, I wished every day that I was someone else. I thought for sure I was the wrong model. I thought differently than everyone else. I did things differently than everyone else. I cared about things in different ways. I was overly passionate about serving others. I was very sensitive. But I could not figure out why I was different. I thought there had to be something wrong with me. As I got older, I started to look for external reasons why I was the way that I was. I was searching for the answers in books, trainings, conferences, coaches, friends, family, television, and any other place I could think of. Then one day I realized something very profound. It was that "thing" inside of me that made me different from others. I had inner magic that made me me.

Rather than denying my true self as I had for years, I started to harness my true self. I started to just be me. I started to snort laugh sometimes because I wanted to. I started to ask the questions I was thinking in my head. I started reaching for the goals and ideas that inspired and excited me. I started to use my inner magic to transform my life.

For too many years, I held a false belief about what I "should" be doing. I literally spent decades of my life on a quest to make everyone else in my life happy. I was not using my gifts and abilities to make a significant change. I was not doing meaningful work. I was just spending all of my energy on trying to please other people. Guess what happened? It didn't work. By the time I was in my early thirties I was exhausted, upset, and blaming everyone else for why I was so unhappy with my life. If you currently feel like this, I completely understand. It's disappointing to feel stuck in your life, and it's frustrating to not feel like you are fulfilling your purpose.

I remember talking with my mom about how frustrated and stuck I was feeling. I even started crying because I was so upset that I'd let it get that bad. I wanted answers. I wanted my purpose. I wanted it NOW! I'm not sure why, but I have little patience. It's truly missing within my body. When

I want something, I don't want to wait for it. I want it right now. Ha!

Anyway, as I was speaking to my mom about my frustrations and then crying, she listened and said, "Allison, do you. Just be you." She then said, "You need to make yourself happy first. You have to do what you were made to do. You have strengths and gifts and you need to start using them. Do it."

After my mom said this, I started crying harder because I knew she was absolutely right. I had been so concerned with taking care of everyone and people-pleasing that I forgot who I was. I completely gave up my identity. I wasn't "me" anymore. I was a mom, a wife, a daughter, a sister, a friend, an entrepreneur, and somehow, I lost the true Allison.

So, how do you start to harness your inner magic? How do you find the power within you? Are there ways to do this? Yes. I'm going to share some of the steps that work well for me when I want to find my inner magic.

Step 1: Discover self-awareness, ask "Who am I?"

I knew that self-awareness was my first step in self-discovery. I decided to start looking for clues every single day. I'd write down ideas on post-it notes. I used a large board in my office to write down all of my dreams and ideas. I started journaling about my ideal life. I wrote down some huge goals. I learned from people who inspired me. I had really deep conversations with my husband and my friends about life.

Eventually, after all of that work, I came up with my purpose statement: *I'm here to empower people to do more, be more, and have more in their lives through designing a life they love.*

If you're feeling stuck, look for the clues. They're there and you just need to notice them.

Ask yourself, "Have I been using my gifts and talents to do meaningful work that aligns with my purpose?" For a long time, I was doing work to distract me from my purpose, and during that time I was feeling unsatisfied in my life.

If you're trying to reach the best version of yourself and want to live a life on purpose, it's critical for you to align what you do best with how you make a living. When I'm speaking or coaching, I like to ask, "What could you do all day long and lose track of time?" That is it! That is the thing that you need to figure out how to do more of.

Step 2: Practice Meditation & Yoga

When I was 16 years old, I started practicing yoga. I've now been in my practice for almost 20 years. The great thing about yoga is that it connects our mind, body, and spirit in miraculous ways. Through the movements and breath, I feel more connected to myself. If I am having a chaotic time in my life, I know that I can pull out my yoga mat and almost instantly connect back to who I am. One of my favorite parts of my yoga classes is the meditation. For those of you who have never meditated, it looks like this. You find a comfortable place to sit. You close your eyes and you focus on your breath. Breathe in, then out, in, then out. As thoughts enter your mind, you kindly release them and then start focusing on your breath again.

This silence connects me to my source. As my mind quiets, I feel a sensation throughout my body. Sometimes I start at the tip of my toes and work my way up to my head, consciously releasing any tension I feel in that area of my body. I feel warmth and release in that area of my body. By the end of this process, my entire body feels light and content. My mind is clear and my soul is happy. Yoga and meditation are powerful tools when you want to connect on a deeper level to yourself. I would highly encourage finding a basic yoga class in your area and try it out. Incorporating a yoga practice into your life can dramatically shift your energy levels and create harmony in your mind, body, and spirit.

Exercise: Stop, Breathe, & Reset

Close your eyes and breathe. This is a self-care technique that you can use anytime and anywhere. Many times, when I'm feeling overwhelmed or stressed, I stop what I am doing, I breathe, and I relax my body. This is a simple way for me to reset myself.

Why does breathing work?

To effectively combat stress, we need to activate the body's natural relaxation response. The "Relaxation Response" was discovered and coined by American Institute of Stress Founding Trustee and Fellow Dr. Herbert Benson. The relaxation response is a physical state of deep rest that changes the physical and emotional responses to stress (e.g., decreases in heart rate, blood pressure, rate of breathing, and muscle tension).

When eliciting the relaxation response:

- *Your metabolism decreases*
- *Your heart beats slower and your muscles relax*
- *Your breathing becomes slower*
- *Your blood pressure decreases*
- *Your levels of nitric oxide are increased*

At American Institute Stress we are often asked, "What is the best way to relieve my stress and relax?" Our typical answer includes an explanation that just as the definition of stress is different for everyone, so are "the best" stress reduction techniques. However, there is one "Super Stress Buster" that evokes the relaxation response that we widely recommend as useful for everyone- even kids. Can you guess what it is? BREATHING! That is right, simply breathing. It is free and can be practiced anywhere- I bet you are even breathing right now! The key, of course, is focused breathing.

The relaxation response is not lying on the couch or sleeping but a mentally active process that leaves the body relaxed, calm, and focused. (Marksberry, 2018)

Step 3: Give Love

On one day I was having a very difficult time in my relationships. I was talking with my coach about how I was so frustrated and angry. I was being very negative. I was sad and disappointed that my life had come to this point. I did not know what to do and I asked my coach what she would do. She encouraged me to give love. Let me tell you, I thought that was the most ridiculous thing I had ever heard in my entire life. GIVE LOVE? Are you kidding me? Give love to the person that lied to me? Give love to the people who told me I couldn't? Give love to the people that wished ill for me? Give love to all of them and then I could feel better? *This has to be wrong*, I thought. *What does she know*, I thought. Well, it seems she was exactly right. I did need to give more love to everyone, including myself. If I wanted to reach my purpose, I needed to first love myself. At this low point in my life, I will admit that I didn't like myself. I blamed myself. I felt guilty, sad, frustrated, and overall like a huge failure to everyone. I hated who I had become. Each and every day I would sit around thinking about what else I hated about myself. I would remind myself of what I did not accomplish. I would compare myself to other people. I would make up reasons for why I should not love myself.

Have you ever gotten to a point of utter

frustration and tried something new just to prove the other person wrong? That's what I did. I thought to myself, *I'll show my coach that she's wrong. Give love. That's crazy. I'll give more love than anyone else I know. I'll give love to the people that have wronged me, lied to me, cheated me, betrayed me, hurt me. But most of all, I'll give love to myself. Each day I will look at myself in the mirror and I'll say, "Allison, I love you." Then to really prove her wrong, I'll add some affirmations because if I try all of these bogus ideas of hers and they don't work... then I'll be right. I can prove her wrong.*

I started my quest to prove my coach wrong. I started slowly at first with my children. I love my children unconditionally, they're easy to love. But I started to love them when they misbehaved, didn't listen, and acted out. I gave them a hug and said simply, "I love you anyways." Then I did it with my husband. He and I were having some difficult things happen in our relationship. At this point, I was very critical of him. I decided I would stop criticizing him, and I would replace it with, "I love you anyways." Day by day I would find more and more people to love. I'd say, "Love ya" to my friends. I'd give my love away by serving people. Eventually, I got in the habit of giving love. I stopped making this a challenge to show my coach how wrong she was, and I began wanting to give love. I wanted to be the most enthusiastic and encouraging person I knew. I wanted to believe in people more than they believed in themselves. I wanted to share ideas, thoughts, goals, and dreams on a bigger level. I wanted to exude love in every situation I met.

I know what you're wondering—what happened? My coach was 100% right. Love transformed me and my life. It's happening right now. I'm sending love to you, my reader. I want amazing and great things in your life. I believe in you. I know you have amazing capabilities. You have no limits. You can do, be, and have anything you want. I give you love.

Exercise: Give Love Challenge

I'd like you to start your own Give Love Challenge in your life. Today, start to give love to yourself, your family, your friends, your colleagues, and even to those people that have wronged you. Start today. Do it. As you give love, you will find the true purpose within you becomes revealed. You will start to operate in a place of love and abundance. Your life will literally change for the better in so many ways. You'll have experiences and people come into your life that you never thought possible. Your light will shine! #givelovechallenge

Step 4: Prioritize Self-Care

Remember, you can't give what you do not have. Self-care is critical to your success. I've heard from so many people who put the needs of everyone else before themselves. Unfortunately, these people often end up very sick. They never took the time to care about themselves and all of that caring for others caused them to neglect the most important thing in their life: their own health. Do you realize that your health is critically important to every single area of your life? If you get really sick tomorrow, would it matter how much money you had? Would it matter what your career was or where you traveled? I bet if you got really sick tomorrow, the only things you would be concerned with is getting better and being with your family.

It was about two years ago when my life went literally and figuratively under construction. During that time, I had so much change happening in my life. Up until that point, I said that I hated change. So, at first, all of this change really was difficult for me. I felt angry, upset, stressed, and in a fog. I wish that I would have understood the concept of self-care during that very difficult time in my life.

Imagine this scene: You are sitting in the office; it's a busy week at work. There's an important meeting you have to prepare for, a large project that you are leading, and your calendar is busy with meetings. Do you take the time to care for yourself? Most people don't. They skip their workout, cancel the fun events, get overworked and stressed out, and then wonder why life feels so draining.

This is one of the worst things you can do. At our financial planning firm, we say to pay yourself first, but I say that even more important than paying yourself first is to take care of yourself first. If you take care of your physical, mental, and emotional health, you're much healthier overall, and this will lead you to have more energy and capacity to deal with the things that life throws at you.

Unfortunately, too many people in the U.S. think that the busier they are, the more successful they will become. All cultures do not have this belief. When my husband and I were in Paris, we were astonished by how cafés did not have to-go cups. We even had a server ask us why we wanted to leave. "You don't have the time?" he asked inquisitively.

In our culture, there is a misconception that if you're really busy, then you're successful. Many people trade their health and well-being by making money. If they spent the time and energy on caring for themselves as well as their careers, they'd feel more fulfilled in all areas of their life.

Exercise: Schedule time for self-care

The items that end up in your calendar are the things you're more likely to do, right? If you want to practice self-care, why not schedule it for yourself? I've found that if I say to myself, "I'm going to work out four times this week," I'm more likely to make the time to work out at least three or four times, if not more. However, on those weeks when I forget to schedule my workout time, then I am least likely to work out at all. Eventually, forgetting to schedule time for myself becomes a routine.

Step 5: Overcome Stress

Did you know that 77% of the U.S. population has said they experience physical signs from stress? Whether it is related to their job, money, worrying, or other fears, stress is a way of life for too many Americans, and it needs to be addressed. (The American Institute of Stress, 2014)

I've been speaking to many people over the past few months. Over and over again I hear about stress, fear, guilt, blame, and feelings of inadequacy. I understand this well because I've had the same feelings. During some of the most difficult times in my life, I've been flooded with stress and fear. These emotions can paralyze us. When I was filled with stress and fear, I was unable to do anything. I would just cycle back to my feelings of fear. I would keep saying things like, "This is so stressful, I'm scared, what will happen, I'm worried, oh my gosh, I can't, I won't!" I would get more negative in my life. I would feel stuck. I would feel unsure. My power was lost. I'm sure you have experienced something similar in your life. You may even be feeling this way right now.

Have you ever said, "I'm having the worst day" and then all of these crazy terrible things start happening? That's typical because you put out the negative thoughts and energy. I recently had one of those days.

– I woke up to 18 inches of snow in Wisconsin in April!

– I spilled coffee on my lap.

– I forgot socks. How did I do that?

– I got stuck in my driveway, got out, and then got stuck in a snowbank along the side of the road.

– I had to prepare for four trainings and events in one day.

– I had a meeting at school to feed more children (this made my heart happy).

The issue with stress, fear, guilt, shame, and worry is that they cause more negative thoughts and experiences to enter our lives. It's interesting because as you start to feel negative, more of the negative comes into your life.

By the end of the day, I was on my treadmill running—which helps me process all the craziness in my life. While I was running, I focused on everything I was grateful for in my life, rather than bemoaning everything that went wrong during the day.

I'm healthy and happy.

My kids are healthy and happy, and very silly.

My husband is so sweet and kind.

My puppy, Juni, kisses me.

My family is wonderful.

I'm surrounded by loving, kind friends.

So, remember, even on those crazy days like mine, there are things to be grateful for.

We all have difficult days. I know that everyone deals with days that don't go as planned. The issue comes in when we stay stuck in this behavior. When we continue to spiral down into the negativity pattern, we feel stuck in our lives.

Exercise: Be Here Now

Today, I'd like you to become more centered on where you are right now. Take a moment to find a quiet location that is free of distractions while you read or listen to this part of the book. Close the door, turn off your computer, and just be here now. Now I'd like you to close your eyes and take a deep breath. Focus on the next 30 minutes we have together. Be here now. So many of us are so busy in our lives that we forget to be present in the moment. Be present. There is no need to think about the future or the past. Right now is all that matters. Being present is something you can do to care for yourself. It's a simple but powerful way to remind yourself to slow down.

Step 6: Start a Gratitude Journal

Cultivate the habit of being grateful for every good thing that comes to you, and to give thanks continuously. And because all things have contributed to your advancement, you should include all things in your gratitude. – Ralph Waldo Emerson

My gratitude journal helps me begin my day more intentionally focused on what I'm grateful for instead of bemoaning what's missing or wrong in my life. Each day when I wake up, I get myself a cup of coffee and write down the things that I'm grateful for in my life. This activity takes less than five minutes, but helps me become more focused on the things that are going right in my life rather than focus on what's wrong or lacking.

Why Gratitude Works

Gratitude is a selfless act. Gratitude acts are done unconditionally to show people that they are appreciated, not because we are looking for something in return. However, that is not to say that people do not return the favor. Gratitude can be contagious in a good

way. Think about some of the happiest people that you know. I bet they are grateful for the good that comes into their lives. – Positive Psychology Program (2017)

Step 7: Go for a walk

How often do we get caught up in the stress in our lives but forget that if we took a break from what we're working on, we'd be able to accomplish so much more? As I was writing about this step, I decided to go for a walk. I know that in my own work it seems that my best ideas come after I've stopped thinking so hard about the situation. It's when I've stopped worrying or lamenting about a challenge that the solution appears with almost no effort at all. Many times in our lives, we want to know now, we want to have the answer now. I've heard that inventor Thomas Edison would take naps or walks in order to figure out solutions to his big inventions. That break from using logical thinking to solve a problem would allow his subconscious brain to help him figure out the solution. I find this happens when I take walks. If I listen to my music while walking, it seems as if the cares of the day just melt away. At the end of my walk, I like to sit in silence and clear my head. Some of the most profound ideas or solutions come in this instance—even without looking for them. Remember to go for a walk!

The best thing happens when we start to tap into our inner magic. I call them #pinchme moments. As I started to use my inner magic to manifest, more and more amazing things in my life, I started to experience a whole bunch of #pinchme moments. These are moments in which I want to pinch myself because I don't know if I'm dreaming or if what I'm experiencing is actually happening.

Remember: Your inner magic will lead you to the exact spot that you are needed. You have all of the greatness you need within you!

You will also start to experience #pinchme moments as you harness your inner magic in your life.

Practicing the Art of Imperfect Action: Questions to Find Your Inner Magic!

Here are some simple ways you can practice self-care to tap into your inner magic. By tapping into your inner magic, you will transform the ways you do everything. You already have the power within you. You have an inner magic that creates miracles. Self-care is so important to your health and well-being. I hope that you will be able to implement one of these ideas into your life.

How to tap into your inner magic:

1. **Start saying affirmations:** Write down "I am" statements about yourself. I've included an exercise in Chapter 4 to find your affirmations. These are the words I want you to repeat to yourself every day. I am _____.

2. **Create a morning ritual:** Get up a half hour earlier each day. During this time, meditate, write in your gratitude journal, and refocus.

3. **Take care of yourself:** Find time to exercise, go for a walk, run, hike, bike ride, or do some activity that you like to do.

4. **Schedule friend time:** I find that I need to schedule friend time as part of my self-care. Every couple of weeks, I spend time with friends, and this fills me up.

5. **Laugh:** Laughter is good for your soul. Have you ever been in a really bad mood, but then something funny happens and

you laugh? How did you feel? Instantly happier. Each day you need to laugh. Find funny jokes, people, or books to read to help you laugh.

6. **Love yourself**! Schedule a massage, manicure or pedicure, get a new outfit, get your hair done, or go on an adventure. Do something for you. If you don't take care of yourself, no one else is going to either. You really need to fill yourself up with the positive experiences that you need. Love yourself.

7. **Find support**: If you're working on yourself, you'll likely need support. Unfortunately, I've found that most people don't have very many people that are very supportive in their lives. That's sad but true. If you need someone to support you in figuring out where you need help, then start looking for it.

8

productivity
hacks that work

*Time is our most precious commodity and yet most of us
live our lives as if we have all the time in the world.* –
Robin Sharma

I could spend one day with you and know
whether or not you are setting yourself up for
success. Each of us has the same amount of time:
24 hours a day, 7 days a week. The difference
between really successful people and those who
are not as successful is how they choose to spend
their time. I'll admit that for years I wasted time
watching TV or doing other unproductive things.

When I put my life under construction, I started studying very successful people. The one common message I heard from all of them is that you need to be in control of your time. If you are allowing other people to dominate how you spend your time, you'll never be successful. As John Maxwell said, "You will never change your life until you change something you do daily."

Each day we have the chance to prepare ourselves for the next day, next week, and next month. I've found that people who are filled with excuses about why they are so busy are really not in control of their time. Many times, these people let unnecessary meetings, errands, unproductive activities, and excuses fill their time. They run around frantically telling everyone how busy they are. But if you evaluated the results of all of their activity, you'd find out that they were not accomplishing much in all of that busy running around. I bet you can clearly picture someone in your life that lets life happen to them. What I've come to realize about this type of person is that they probably have never been taught to manage their time. So, if this describes you, there is hope!

Note: I am not suggesting that if you want to be a success, you are not able to have fun. I'm simply suggesting that you may need to schedule your fun and not let the fun times exceed the work time and vice versa.

Start with Yourself

I'm going to share something a little embarrassing. When I started trying to be more successful at managing my time, I wasn't focusing on me. I was actually pointing at everyone else around me and sharing why I thought they needed to be more productive. EEK! Don't do this. The one person that I did this with the most was my husband. Tony and I own a business together, so I thought it was my duty to explain all of the ways that he could improve his time management and productivity. For a long time, I would suggest how he could do this or that better. Guess what? This did not work.

Now I understand that I can't worry about fixing everyone else. I need to put my time and energy toward fixing myself first. As Mahatma Gandhi said, "Be the change you want to see in the world." I started to work on myself because I now understood this critical point. If I want to help someone else change, I need to model what it looks like first. Just telling someone to do something else when I'm not doing it doesn't make much sense.

How do you find the time?

As I speak to more and more people from around the world since finishing my first book, *Life Under Construction: Designing a Life You Love*, I'm constantly asked this question: "How do you find the time to do all of that?"

Specifically, people will ask me these types of questions.

- When do you find the time to do your work?
- When do you find the time to write an entire book with two young children?
- When do you find the time to practice your speech?
- To prepare? To plan? To promote? To write? To design? To create?

These are all great questions and all funnel into the main question of how you find the time to do what you want to do.

For many years, I made excuses for why I didn't have enough time to accomplish each and every one of those things. Guess what happened when

I made excuses? I didn't do anything because I found reasons why I didn't have enough _____. (I used to fill in the blank with words like time, energy, ideas, or focus.) One day I realized that the excuses would only get me more excuses. So, I decided to stop. Then I told myself that I do have the time, resources, and abilities to figure it out. My husband says that I'm an expert at compartmentalizing my tasks. If I'm working on editing my book, then I'm working on just that. If I am at home with the children, then I'm at home with the children. Obviously, there comes a time when I do have to do more than one thing at a time, but I've found I'm much less productive when I try to do too many things at once. I would sneak away after the kids went to sleep, wake up really early, write during the day, and do whatever I needed to do to make it work.

One day I received something very special in the mail. It represented my new thought process. My new view about accomplishing something. It represented over a year of my life. My first book proof arrived. That was a surreal day. I remember being SO excited to open the box. My eyes teared up when I saw the cover and felt the book. My sense of accomplishment was overwhelming. I was proud of myself. I did it!

Evaluate Your Time

If you are not experiencing the results in the life that you would like, you may want to evaluate how you are spending your time and energy. One easy way to do this is to track your activities for one week. You can do this every hour or half hour. Write down what you worked on and be as specific as possible. If you had a call, write down who it was with, what it was about, and what the result was.

Then, at the end of the week, look at how you spent your time. You'll likely see that a lot of your time was spent on activities that do not give you the results that you're seeking. That's okay. By becoming more self-aware of how you spend your time, you're already on track to improvement. Nice job!

Make Time for What Matters

Maybe you tell yourself that you don't have the time. By simply reframing this question for yourself too, "How can I MAKE the time?" you'll find that you are able to get much more accomplished. Have you ever heard about the Pareto Principle? In 1906, Italian economist

Vilfredo Pareto noted that 80% of Italy's land was owned by 20% of the people (Kruse, 2016). He became somewhat obsessed with this ratio, seeing it in everything. For example, he observed that 80% of the peas in his garden came from 20% of his pea plants.

You can also apply this principle to your priorities. For example, 80% of your time should be spent on the 20% of the priorities that give you the most results. John Maxwell teaches that "the greatest detriment to your success is doing too many things and doing the wrong things." Think about what you do every single day. Are you experiencing the results in the life that you would like? If not, how can you make time for what matters to you?

How to Find More AMAZING Ideas :

1. **Expect that great ideas will come to you.** *Note: Remember that every idea you have is a gift. Embrace it as a gift.

2. **Write down your great ideas.** Find a piece of paper, your phone, or ask someone to text you the idea.

3. **Think about the great idea.** Some questions

you may want to ask yourself are: Why is this a great idea? Who could this great idea help? What makes me excited about this great idea? How could I use this great idea? When should I work on this great idea?

4. **Make a plan.** As soon as you get enough of an idea that you want to pursue this great idea, create a plan of action for yourself. You may have gaps in this plan, but fill it out as well as you can with the information you already know. If you have questions, feel free to write them down for yourself. Somehow they will get answered.

5. **Take imperfect action.** This means taking a step toward your great idea. Any small step will make an impact.

6. **Be okay with failure.** Some of the steps you take toward your goal may not work how you anticipated. This is okay. Remember you are learning something new. You will not know how; if you knew how you would have already done it. Learn from failure, improve, and then try again.

7. **Anticipate the amazing result.** If you want to have amazing results on your idea, you need to start with the mindset that it will be amazing from the start. As you set this intention, that will happen. However, if you question yourself, put

negative energy toward it, or expect it to fail—often times it will. Anticipate the results that will lead to the most good and they will happen.

Plan and Succeed

I suggest that you use a planner while you are working on becoming more diligent about how you spend your time. I like a planner that shows each day and also tracks hour by hour what I need to be doing. This allows me to be very proactive about prioritizing my time. I would like to challenge you to sit down next week on Sunday night or Monday morning with your planner. Here's what to do:

1. **Start with you.** First, write down all of the events you already have scheduled for yourself that are not work-related. (This might include working out, lunches with friends, hair appointments, etc.)

2. **Family.** Now I want you to write down all of the activities you have scheduled for your family.

3. **Work/Career Goals.** Start with a list of three things that are most important for you to accomplish this week that will give you the most results. For example, one of

my mentors asked me, "What is your one big goal for the week?" That week I needed to prepare a presentation for a few trainings I had coming up, so that was my big goal for the week. By accomplishing this goal, I knew that I would feel better prepared for my trainings, and I'd have time to practice the presentation.

4. **Work/Career Project Time.** Write down the time that you need to accomplish those three big goals you just wrote down for yourself. Chunk time and allow yourself adequate time for revisions, edits, etc. Remember, these goals will likely provide you the results that you want, so taking the time to work on them is important to your success.

5. **Work/Career Meetings.** Last, and probably least, I'd like you to schedule meetings. Before any meeting or calls, I want you to set your intention for the meeting by asking yourself, "What do I hope to gain from this interaction?" If you can't find a reason for the meeting, perhaps you should either cancel or reschedule the meeting. I've found that if

I wanted to, I could spend 99% of my time sitting at meetings. For a long time, I thought this was a useful way to spend my time because I was networking. Then I realized that I wasn't actually reaching my goals and dreams by sitting in meetings because I wasn't taking action. Sitting in meetings or going to a bunch of networking events was actually an excuse for me to stay busy and not accomplish my goals.

6. **Review your week.** What are the top three things that you need to accomplish each day to reach your goals? Write these down.

7. **Track your results.** At the end of the week, track your results. Did you accomplish more this week? Did you feel more productive? Do you feel like you're moving in the right direction?

By implementing this productivity system into your routine, you'll soon find that you've accomplished more goals.

BOOM! With these productivity hacks, you'll be reaching your goals.

Practicing the Art of Imperfect Action:
Questions to Help You be More Productive!

Creating a personal growth plan for yourself can be a great way to help you focus on what's most important. I've done this in my own life, and it has been effective in helping me grow and be more productive. After I created a personal growth plan, I was able to focus on the activities that would give me the best results in my personal and professional life. By having them all written down for myself, I was able to plan my weeks more intentionally and use my time in the most efficient ways possible.

Your personal growth plan starts off simply by asking these questions:

1. Who are you? (Idea: take a personality test and look at your strengths.)
2. What areas do you want to grow in?
3. What resources will you use to help you grow?
4. How will you stay accountable?
5. Why is this important to you?

That's it! It can all be contained on one piece of

paper when you start. As you think and research more about your growth, your personal growth plan will likely become longer and more involved.

9

crushing self-doubt: you are worth it!

Doubt kills more dreams than failure ever will. – Suzy Kassem

I recently had an exciting, but oh-so-scary opportunity present itself, and I thought, "This really scares me, but I really, really want to do it." I thought about it more and then I asked myself these questions:

1. Am I fearful of this because it's outside my comfort zone? (YES!)

2. If I do it, will I be helping someone else? (YES!)
3. If I do this, will it provide me with an opportunity to learn something I've never learned before? (YES!)
4. Will I be in harm's way if I do this? (Possibly, then I did a Google search. This did not help me. Never Google something scary before you do it. HA!)
5. Will I be in unknown situations with unknown people? (Absolutely.)
6. If I don't do this, will I always think about what could have happened? (Absolutely.)

After asking myself these questions, I realized that I HAD to do this and that I couldn't wait. I needed to do it and figure out the rest later. Have you ever had opportunities like this come up in your life? Things that are scary and exciting at the exact same time? Things that make you wonder?

I bet you're wondering what this "thing" was! I signed up to go on a transformational leadership trip with my mentor John Maxwell and his team of coaches.

Oh, my goodness. Just saying that freaks me out. I'm really doing it. One hundred of us John

Maxwell Team members went with John Maxwell to Paraguay in September 2017 to train 15,000 people.

I wrote this when I was facing one of my fears. I had a large amount of self-doubt. It wasn't the same type of self-doubt that I had faced for years. It was fear of the unknown. I wanted to share it because this is how I thought about it. I was excited about the opportunity, and I let the excitement and hope be more than the doubts. As you start to do things out of your comfort zone, you will likely have these types of opportunities happen too. You may want to ask yourself similar questions.

For a long time, self-doubt was part of my daily routine. I woke up in the morning, and I would go into the bathroom to brush my teeth. Then the self-doubt would just wash over me. It would wash over me and flood my brain with doubt. I would doubt my abilities to do, be, or have what I wanted in my life. In the back of my mind, I was always thinking, "Allison, are you kidding me? They're going to find out who you really are." I would question myself all day every day. I was so hard on myself. I was a perfectionist. I could see the good in other people, but for some reason, I had told myself that I was not good enough. I was never good enough. I recently heard that everyone has two main fears. One is "I am not enough." And the other fear is "I will not be loved."

Guess what I realized about all of this self-doubt I was feeling? IT WAS FAKE! The terrible doubts that were flooding into my head were all fake. They were stories that I had made up in my head years ago, and they were not real. They were fake stories that I needed to let go.

When I was experiencing a lot of self-doubts, it was directly correlated to my low self-confidence.

Believe in Yourself

From my own experience, I want to say that you should follow your heart, and the mind will follow you. Believe in yourself, and you will create miracles. – Kailash Satyarthi

Believing in your own potential is a critical piece of tapping into your inner magic. Do you realize that your potential is limitless? That means that you can do, be, or have whatever you want. You can design the life that you love. As soon as you truly believe this, you can start to create the vision of what you want in your life. There are some people that may disagree with the statement "you have no limits." I am not one of them. I've experienced having no limits first hand.

Valuing Yourself

Until you value yourself, you won't value your time. Until you value your time, you will not do anything with it. – M. Scott Peck

I needed to value myself. I needed to know that I was worth it. I needed to understand that I had something to offer the world. For years I had been conditioned to think that I was bragging if I mentioned something that I did well. I wasn't supposed to talk about the things that I could do better than other people. I was supposed to be humble. I was encouraged to talk about all of the negative things that were happening to me. I could talk about how it was so difficult, or how I struggled. Think for a moment about your childhood. Were you encouraged to talk about what you did well or what you struggled at?

For years I had to try to hold a good image of myself inside of me. I had awesome ideas. I was creative. I loved singing, dancing, performing, art, and athletics. I was in the talented and gifted program. I had all of these amazing things going for me and yet I never felt like I was enough. I felt unsure of myself most of the time. I had learned that I shouldn't talk about the awesome things that were happening. Instead, I was encouraged to talk about what I was going to do to get better—because I wasn't enough. I was never enough. I needed to work on that constantly. I needed to read, study, research, and grow. I needed to be more.

Have you ever felt that you needed to be more? Or have you ever felt that constant pull to move or take action in order to gain approval? If so, I completely understand. I was there. This was my reality for over thirty years. Until that day when my friend pulled me aside at the coffee shop and said that I was enough just as I was. On that day, I needed the reassurance from her that I could let go of all of the perfectionism I was holding onto. I was enough. I didn't have to prove anything. She would accept me for just being me. That day was a turning point in my life. I'd never had someone tell me that. Don't get me wrong, I felt loved by others. I have been blessed with so much love from my family and friends. However, on that day, my dear friend saw through to my low of self-confidence and what it was doing to my broken spirit . She understood how my lack of self-confidence was holding me back from becoming who I really wanted to become. It was also holding me back from doing what I really wanted to do. Self-doubt cripples you by keeping you stuck in a life that you didn't choose. Your skewed ideas, while faced with self-doubt, manipulate what you think you can do, be, or have in your life.

I'm beyond grateful for my friend for stepping up and seeing me for what I was doing to myself. On that day, my friend Angie gave me permission to kick the self-doubt out of my head. She gave me some interesting words to use when I felt the doubt flooding in. She said to me, "Allison, whenever you feel that way say... 'I'm not listening to this anymore. I'm AWESOME.'" Then she said she would remind me if I ever forgot this. I needed that because I am awesome, and so are you! (Be this person for your friends and family too. We all need someone that will be that person for us.)

When was the last time you screamed at the top of your lungs, "I AM SO AWESOME!"?

Try it. Stop right now. Go out to your car and scream to yourself, "I AM SO AWESOME!"

I cried the first time I did that. It felt so unreal. I

had been beating myself up internally for so many years that as I said the words, inside I knew I didn't truly believe them. Yet.

The Power of YET!

Yet is another powerful word when you are overcoming self-doubt. Many times, if you lack self-confidence, it's because you have something that you want to do but you haven't started because you don't know how or you're feeling lost. At these times in life, all you need to do is add the word "YET" to the end of whatever it is that you are working on next. For example, you could say, "I don't work out...YET." The YET implies you may not do that right now, but you are going to start. Sometimes that is all that it takes to get you ready to make a significant change in your life. YET is a powerful way to transform what you are doing and step into what you want to do.

Remember: You are enough. Believe in yourself. I believe in you!

Practicing the Art of Imperfect Action:
Questions for Kicking Out Self-Doubt!

This is an important exercise. Please take time to complete it. Before you start, find a quiet location to work. You will need a piece of paper and a pen. Turn off all of your electronics and any notifications on your phone and computer. Set the timer on your phone for 30 minutes.

1. Close your eyes and take a deep clarifying breath. While you are breathing in, say these words out loud, "Let," breath out, "Go." Do this 10 times.

Now open your eyes and focus on these questions:

1. What are the limiting beliefs or stories that I have been telling myself that have caused me to doubt myself?
2. What has been holding me back?
3. Why do I doubt myself?
4. What is stopping me from being the best version of me?
5. Let it go! When you feel that you have written down every single story and limiting belief that has caused you to doubt yourself, tear up or burn the piece of paper. These are fake stories that you

have been holding on for too long. You are not these limiting beliefs. You are not these fake stories.

6. I am so AWESOME. I want you to repeat these words to yourself:

"I will lead my life. I will believe in myself and my abilities. I will create. I am unique. I am awesome. I am exactly what this world needs. I am FABULOUS. I am ENOUGH! I AM AWESOME!!!"

A note about releasing emotions: This can be a very impactful experience. It's okay to cry, yell, and feel angry. Allow yourself to feel the emotions that bubble up as the stories emerge. It's okay. This is an important part of the process. You are releasing these stories. You are releasing the emotions that have kept you stuck for so long.

Reflect on how you feel. Once again, close your eyes and breathe in deeply. Note how your body and mind feel. You probably feel lighter and your mind feels calm and relaxed. You may feel a bit low on energy because you just released a lot of things from your body. Right now would be a great time to go outside and take a walk.

Congratulations. You did it! You are kicking

self-doubt out of your life. This was a big step for you. By going through this process, you probably had thoughts and ideas come up that you may have been repeating over and over again in your head.

By releasing all of these limiting beliefs, you are going to be able to move forward. Those doubts are gone. They have no power over you. You are not those stories. You are not those limiting beliefs. You are not that negative self-image. You are awesome!

10

go all in

You can't go back and change the beginning, but you can start where you are and change the ending. – C.S. Lewis

I've heard that at the end of life, people were asked what their greatest regret was, and the number one thing they said was to have the courage to live the life they dreamt of. Imagine spending your entire life waiting. Waiting for the time to be right, to feel like it, or to have all of the circumstances fall into alignment. Let me tell you a secret: it's never going to be the right time.

No matter how long you wait, the timing will never work perfectly, you won't ever feel like it, and none of the circumstances will fall into alignment. Right now is the perfect time to courageously step up to your greatness. You already have everything within you to start. Many times, we set crazy huge goals for ourselves and then we get stuck because we don't know how to move forward. For the longest time, when I didn't know how to do something, I quit. I thought that if I didn't know how, that meant that I shouldn't do it. If I didn't have all of the answers, that meant that I wasn't going to be successful.

Then I found out that truly successful people just start, even when they only know a small part of how to achieve their goal.

Life happens. Success will not be easy.

As soon as you make the decision to go all in, life happens. Every time I declared that something was going to happen and I started to chase that goal, life came up. When life comes up, it can sometimes deter us from doing that thing we want to do. It can stop us because life's interruptions can throw us off course. When I was writing my last book, *Life Under Construction: Designing a Life You Love,* my life was literally and figuratively under construction. Things exploded in my life, which was difficult and scary. I could have easily told myself that this was the sign that I should not chase that goal to write my book or that the timing wasn't right. At this time, I had a brand new baby, and I wasn't sleeping much. I was helping my mom go through cancer treatments, I was building a house, multiple businesses, and I was trying to grow myself. To say the timing wasn't ideal is an understatement. Many people would have given up had they been faced with one of these obstacles. I won't lie—there were days when I wanted to give up, but I didn't because I knew deep down that this is exactly what we face when we go all in.

If you want to step into your greatness, you need to recognize that life will get harder before it gets easier. – Allison Liddle

Life will throw new obstacles, bigger than anything you've ever faced before. Opportunities will also come to you. The opportunities may be scary as well. The people that start to enter your life will amaze and astound you. On your quest to design a life you love and go all in, you'll start to have things fall into place.

As I was speaking to my friend Sid Samuels, owner of the commercial construction contractor group Samuels Group, Inc ., he shared the roller coaster effect that many of us experience in business and life. He described it like this: There are times in your business or life when you feel like you are at the top of a roller coaster. At those times, you and your team are excited, positive, and feel successful. Unfortunately, there are other times when maybe business switches, you lose a great employee, or something happens, and now you're heading down that same rollercoaster screaming the whole way. At the bottom of the ride, you feel some fear and you wonder how you'll build it back up. It's at moments like this that you need something to help you move forward. You need hope to understand that you'll go back up the rollercoaster. You'll meet success again. Ultimately things will work out. Your job is to surround yourself with people that will go on this life ride with you and want the success as much as you do. This is a critical understanding of success. It will not be easy. There are some people that can't handle this process. The sooner you can realize that it will be a ride, the sooner you'll meet success and achieve your goals.

If you knew how, you would have already done it.

When I was working on finishing up my first book, I remember feeling so overwhelmed by what I didn't know. For days, I would lament about everything I didn't know about publishing a book. Then one day I shifted my thoughts to the things I did know... today. I would ask myself, "What is the one thing I could do today to move closer to my goal? What could I do that would push me forward, even just a baby step?" That would be the next thing I would work on. Eventually, as I gained momentum in working toward my goal, I realized that my energy shifted and the coolest things started to happen. I was in flow and working on my purpose. In doing so, the answers that I needed to figure out began coming to me organically. To analytical people, this may seem bogus. It did to me at first too. As I was in flow, the answers came to me in such a way that I could not even explain how it was happening. The people, resources, book ideas, and events came to me without too much effort. I would look for signs that I was on the right path by simply asking the question, "What should I do next?" There were days when I would set up a call to talk with someone new, a complete stranger. I would get on the phone with them, and I would ask them a few questions to get the conversation started, and then almost magically I'd find out that they either knew my next step or knew the person who could help me with the next step.

During a recent coaching call, one of my clients asked me this great question: "Allison, what do I do if I've been pre-programmed to look at everything in black and white? I'm a very analytical person. It's difficult for me to give up knowing how." I loved this question because I have felt the exact same way for much of my life. It was difficult for me to truly give up the how. I remember times when I would be talking about my next dream or goal with a friend of mine, and he would say, "Allison you're trying to figure out the how. Stop it." I would laugh and realize that was what I was doing. I needed to suspend my need to know how. I needed just to take the next best step. I'm not suggesting that you can't have a plan of the items that you do know right now, but I'd like you to be open to the fact that many of the how questions that you want to be answered may not be clear right away. This feels uncomfortable for most of us, and that is why many people quit before they even start. They think that if they don't know how then they can't do it. This is not true. You may not know the how. You will not be 100% sure. I'd recommend getting comfortable with being uncomfortable.

Visualize Yourself "Going All In!"

Have you ever gone *all in* on something? When I ran track in middle school, I had a phenomenal coach. He would encourage me to go all in at practice. He'd talk with me before practice as we were stretching and tell us that we needed to practice like we wanted to perform. He knew that the majority of being successful at anything in life was to mentally prepare to *go all in*.

I've heard that if you motivate the mind, the body will follow. Take the time to motivate your mind. Take the time to visualize the positive outcome you want. Take the time to see yourself achieving the goal and becoming exactly who you want to be. If you want to lose 10 pounds, visualize yourself already there. Tell yourself that you have already accomplished it. It seems a little bit strange until you realize that your subconscious mind gives you anything that you tell it. If you continue to tell it that you are fat, lazy, and a terrible eater, guess what your brain will do? It will show you ways to continue to be fat, lazy, and a terrible eater. The brain does what the brain knows. All you need to do is reprogram what you're telling it.

Imagine that you tell yourself that you are healthy, strong, you work out, you make healthy food choices, and you weigh _ (whatever 10 pounds lighter is). Guess what your brain will do? It will help encourage you to become that new version of yourself because it thinks that you already are!

Thoughts are Things

Choose your thoughts carefully. Have you ever heard that thoughts are things? What you think about you get more of. If you think negative thoughts, negative things come to you. If you think positive thoughts, positive things come to you. Newton's Third Law of physics is: for every action there is an equal and opposite reaction (Newton's third law, 2018). If that is true, then for everything good that you put out there, you will have an equal amount of good coming back at you. This can also be referred to as the law of cause and effect. The reverse is true as well. For anything negative you put out there, the same negativity will inevitably come back to you. Just think about the last bad day you had. Maybe you spilled coffee, or the dog chewed your shoe—and then what did you say to yourself? This is going to be a bad day. The next thing you know, you had someone cut you off in traffic, you forgot to prepare for an important meeting, and your entire day was ruined. However, now imagine that you decided after that first bad thing happened, you would choose a different attitude. You decided consciously that you would not let that ruin your day and that today was going to be so awesome. You would change the trajectory of your whole life. Things would fall into place. Your day would go much better.

Remember: Thoughts are things.

**Practicing the Art of Imperfect Action:
Questions to Help You Go All In**
Here are questions I'd like you to ponder.

1. What if I went ALL IN for the next 90 days?

2. What could change in my life?

3. Who would I be helping?

4. What is the thing that scares me the most right now? What am I most afraid to start? That is the next thing I need to go all in on.

5. Many of us have so many stories about why something can't work. What if we put all of our energy into why it will work? List all the reasons your next big thing will work.

In 90 days a lot can change (or not). Why not try? What do you have to lose?

what's your definition of success?

With success, my influence is limited; with significance, my influence is unlimited. – John C. Maxwell

I recently had the honor of keynote speaking at the Financial Literacy Conference in central Wisconsin. After my speech, I had a man come up and say, "I've studied all of those motivational speakers and authors. I've read the books, watched their videos, and I wonder how do you define success?"

I never imagined that I would have someone

come and ask me that question. I stopped and thought about success for a moment. I don't really like that word: success. I've learned from my mentor John Maxwell that as soon as you taste significance, success will never satisfy. I believe that success is a piece of the puzzle, but I've decided to create a different puzzle out of my life and have committed to lead a life of significance.

When I explained this to this man, he looked at me confused. I explained more, "I've had some of the most significant moments in my life in the past few months. During these times, I've realized that money, possessions, and achievement didn't matter to me anymore. I knew that I was successful when I shared my gifts, and they helped someone move forward in some area of his or her life."

For example, what if something in my keynote speech encouraged someone to take action in their life? What if they stopped criticizing themselves? What if they finally started their first business? What if they took more time to play with their child? What if they gained more meaning in their life? That would be a win for me. Do I get anything directly from them having a change in their life? Nope. However, the more I add value to other people, the more I feel like I'm contributing to helping people. I love the messages I get almost daily from people taking action in their life. Last week, my friend Joy decided to start her first business and said I inspired her. The week before, a friend started writing their book and another changed jobs. My clients and colleagues have to start their speaking careers or even recorded a video when they felt too nervous to do that before. When I can have this kind of an impact on the lives and careers of others, that is leading a life of significance. I LOVE THIS!

The more I focus on using my gifts to add value to the lives of others, the more opportunities, people, and the amazing experiences that I have. These are what I call "pinch me" experiences. I can't explain it other than I feel like I'm on the path of significance. I'm working in my strength zone to make a bigger impact. To help more people. To share what has worked and not worked in my own life.

The man looked at me and smiled. He thanked me and walked away, but I felt that I'd receive a message soon from him about some change he made within himself that day.

Each of us has a different definition of success. Have you ever written down what you believe success means to you? I've met so many people that may have material wealth, but still feel like they don't have the love they want. I've met people that love their career, but don't have something else. Success is so different for each of us and I think it all comes down to you figuring out what fulfills your heart. Here are some questions that may help you uncover what success means to you and what will ultimately fulfill your life's purpose.

The Art of Imperfect Action Success Questions
Success starts with knowing your purpose for life. If you don't know your purpose, it will be difficult to be a success in life. – John C. Maxwell

1. **What is my purpose?** Identifying your giftedness, strengths, and passion will help you determine your purpose. For the longest time, I said, "I'm confused about my purpose." Guess what happened? I got even more confused. Then one day I had a friend share this powerful idea. She said, "Allison, you do know your purpose. Just start looking for the clues." I did that. I would look for the things that excited me and energized me. Then I'd write them down. Eventually, I figured out that my purpose is to "empower people

to do more, be more, and have more to design lives they love."

2. How do I define success? After you determine your purpose, you need to think about how you define success. How will you know when you've achieved success? What do you need to fulfill your life's purpose?

3. How can I grow myself? Now you know your purpose and how you define success—the next piece of the puzzle is to figure out how to grow yourself in your purpose. Focus on becoming the best version of yourself in that area. For example, if you are a teacher and you know that your purpose is to teach our next generation, then you want to find resources to grow yourself in your teaching abilities. Who would be the best person for you to learn from? What training, books, or certifications could you get to improve your teaching? One of the main things that people ask when they start off on the growth journey is, "How long is this going to take?" John Maxwell says it's better to ask yourself, "How far will I go?" Growth is a journey.

4. **Am I adding value to the lives of others?** If you want to multiply your efforts, you must add value to the most people possible. Adding value means using your purpose to positively impact others. For me, this means writing this book and making it the best I can possibly make it. I know that if I do this, I will positively impact you, my reader. When I wrote my first book, I was amazed at the number of kind messages I received about how my book helped people in their lives. I know that when I add value to more and more people, I will reach success because I am fulfilling my purpose of sharing what I've learned to help others. Think about your own purpose. Do you intentionally find ways to add value to others? Selfish people may reach monetary success, but they will not have anyone around to help them enjoy it. The best path to success is by helping more and more people reach success as well.

5. **Who do I have surrounding me?** Motivational speaker Jim Rohn said, "You are the average of the five people you spend the most time with." After I read this quote, I was very choosy about who I surrounded myself with.

6. **What are my strengths?** You cannot and should not be good at everything. We all have some limitations. Successful people understand this concept and choose the top two to three things that they do extremely well and focus on those things... ONLY. Then they find other people to help them with everything else. If you are starting off on your success journey, it may be difficult for you to find help, but start looking. I'm sure if you really thought about it, you could find someone in your life right now that could help you. Focusing on your strengths will transform how quickly you are able to grow yourself. Most people focus on fixing themselves. If they would focus their energies on growing in their strengths, they'd exceed their expectations.

These success questions can radically transform how you experience your life.

Stories of Significance and Success

In the fall of 2017, I traveled over the equator with my mentor John Maxwell and a team of coaches to conduct transformational leadership change in Paraguay. Within one week, 100 coaches trained over 15,000 people in Paraguay on values-based leadership, and this has now resulted in over 120,000 people in that country being trained. During this trip, I met some of the kindest and most compassionate leaders. These leaders come from diverse experiences and backgrounds. However, the one thing I believe ties them together is an experience of success, unlike anything they have experienced before while they served as a leadership coach in Paraguay. These are their stories of how they define success.

I want to thank Gloria Burgess, Ph.D. and Barbara Gustavson for sharing their thoughtful perspectives about how to define success with us. Thank you so much, my friends!

Paraguay's Landfill Harmonic Orchestra Success

By Gloria J. Burgess, PhD | CEO & Founder, Jazz International | Executive Director & Founder, The Lift Every Voice Foundation

I returned to Paraguay for two reasons. First, I wanted to witness and experience firsthand the work I had begun the previous year. As part of a cadre of 200+ coaches, we were invited to lift up leaders and equip them to introduce life-giving values in a culture that desperately desired healing and deep transformation.

Secondly, I wanted to reunite with another leader who is transforming the Paraguayan culture through the power of music—one person at a time and one piece of garbage at a time. His name is Favio Chávez. Favio conceived, created, and now directs La Orquesta de Instrumentos Reciclados de Cateura, popularly known as the Landfill Harmonic Orchestra or Los Reciclados. Favio works with Nicolás Gómez, or Colá as he likes to be called. A former carpenter, Colá now makes musical instruments for the orchestra.

Prior to creating this unusual ensemble, Favio was an environmental engineer. He worked at an enormous landfill adjacent to the community his pupils call home. Realizing that trash could be revitalized and given another purpose, Favio sought out Colá to salvage discarded oil cans, drain pipes, bottle caps, keys, and assorted utensils to fashion these items and other refuse into violins, violas, cellos, wind instruments, and more for the children to play. Thus began a journey and labor of love. From its very humble beginnings in the tiny, close-knit community of Cateura, Los Reciclados now travels the world, sharing music and goodwill wherever they go. Indeed, the motto of this amazing musical ensemble is: *The world sends us its garbage, we send back music.*

But that's not all.

Before the landfill gave birth to the orchestra, the children of Cateura were destined to an intergenerational lifestyle of extreme poverty, a life where drug use is rampant and early teen pregnancy is the norm. With the opportunity to become part of the orchestra, the girls and boys can now begin to envision a different way of life.

Favio and Colá hold the vision for a brighter future not only for the young people who are members of the orchestra but also for their families and the community of Cateura. In fact, the orchestra is only one pillar of a much bigger strategy. In addition to infusing their world with music, the overarching plan also includes assisting orchestra members with their scholastic work, supporting orchestra members in obtaining their first job by working on behalf of Los Reciclados, and providing better housing for the families. In this way, Favio and Colá are building a sturdy bridge that, when the musicians and their families walk on it, can transform their lives right here right now for this generation and for generations to come. Not only are these visionary leaders equipping youth for transformation in the small, land-locked country of Paraguay, but Favio, Colá, and the young, talented musical artists in Los Reciclados are transforming the hearts, minds, and souls of audiences around the world.

Understanding Success Is Not All Or Nothing

By Barbara Gustavson, President & Executive Coach, Discover Next Step, Executive Director, John Maxwell Team, DiscoverNextStep.com

Prior to Paraguay, I had been struggling with some scary health issues. Normally I would stay back and wait until I was completely well as I never like to be a burden or slow things down, but for this trip, I felt something burning inside that I needed to be there.

I discovered that even though I had some limitations and couldn't go out to every roundtable, I can still be effective, live in my purpose, and help others. It didn't have to be an "all or nothing" thing. I could set healthy parameters with my self-care, then other times I could be "all in"in facilitating roundtables and going to the events. And it was okay to say no to going out at times and taking the time I needed to recover.

It's crazy that it took me going halfway across the world to learn this, but it changed how I viewed my success. It wasn't anymore about accomplishments or doing things "big." Instead, it was taking what I had and giving with my heart while planting seeds of growth and compassion for others.

Remember: success looks differently for everyone. You need to define this for yourself.

Practicing the Art of Imperfect Action:
Questions to Help You Define Success for Yourself

Every single person on the planet defines success in a different way. Your definition is unique to you. What you want to achieve and be is different and that is okay. Once you realize that success is a personal journey of becoming the best version of yourself, the success journey becomes one of significance.

1. What is my purpose? *Identifying your giftedness, strengths, and passion will help you determine your purpose.*

2. How do I define success? *Create a list of all of the words that you think relate to success. Then circle the three that excite you the most. How could you write a definition of success using those words?*

3. How can I grow myself? *Success leaves clues, you need to find other people that have done what you want to do and find out how they did it.*

4. Am I adding value to the lives of others? *Describe specifically who you are helping.*

5. Who do I have surrounding me? *You need supportive people.*

6. What are my strengths? *What are the things you do better than other people? These are your strengths.*

believe you can
and you will

Whether you think you can, or you think you can't—you're right. – Henry Ford

You are meant to make a significant difference with your life. You are meant to believe in yourself. Your life is a great adventure. You are not an accident. You were meant for much more than you can even imagine. Believe in your power. Believe that you already have everything you need for greatness.

Do you want to have more success in any area of your life? Do you want to feel more content?

Do you want to be happier? Do you want to experience peace of mind? Do you want to create a vision for what a great life would look like?

Motivation comes from filling yourself with the right type of energy. Motivation is taking the next right step, moving a little bit closer to your next goal. Doing the thing that you keep questioning in your head if you can or can't do. Deciding that you are not going to "give-up" but instead you are going to put all of your energy into "going up."

I did not understand this concept when I was younger. I did not realize how negative energy impacted me. Negative energy comes into your life in different ways. As I thought more and more about this, I developed the idea of the "Hot Air Balloon Effect."

I currently live in a beautiful community in central Wisconsin. We have lakes, rivers, rolling hills, farmland, and a mountain. It's a magical place, but there is one other thing that makes it even more magical... hot air balloons!

During the summer months, you will often see a hot air balloon floating along the horizon. It's a fun surprise, and they always fill me with happiness. Over the past months, I've been privileged to speak to thousands of people from all over the world. After each of my speeches, there is one question I get every single time, and it made me realize what the questions and the hot air balloons have in common.

I've heard this question from CEOs of successful companies and students in third-world countries. I've heard it from professionals with credentials and people that did not finish high school. Race, age, gender, religion, and demographics do not matter. This question is universal and global—so I'm going to address it.

The question is: What if I lack the self-confidence to do _____? (Fill in the blank with whatever your goal is.)

The answer is the "Hot Air Balloon Effect." Imagine for a moment that you are a hot air balloon. You are simply floating along enjoying your glorious life. You feel happy, content, and fulfilled. You are working to fulfill your purpose. As you float along, you would need something to keep yourself floating in the air, right? You would need to be filled with warmth and positive energy to lift you higher—or hot air. As you fill yourself with more of the hot air and positive energy, you would reach heights higher than you could imagine. You'd see farther than you ever did before. Your perspective would change. The small things that mattered little in your life would slowly fade into the distance. Your life purpose would be much bigger!

Now imagine that you stopped filling yourself with hot air. If you turned off the positive energy and thoughts, what would happen to your hot air balloon? It would likely fall. It would fall slowly at first and then more quickly. The trees and obstacles would scare you. You'd feel like you lost control of your hot air balloon. Or would you?

All you need to do to lift yourself higher is to turn back on the hot air and positive energy. As soon as you do this, guess what happens almost immediately? You begin to rise up higher and higher almost effortlessly. Your mood lightens, your perspective changes, and your life floats along once again.

So, how do you have more self-confidence? Fill yourself with positive energy. Ask yourself: "Does this lift me higher or drag me down?" If it's not lifting you higher, it's dragging you down, and life will become more difficult. If you want to live with more self-confidence, choose to lift yourself higher!

Today, harness the energy of your hot air

balloon by believing that you can. Do you see yourself as a success or a failure? If you believe that you are a success, your brain will believe it. If you feel like you are a failure, your brain will believe that as well. Belief, therefore, is the first step in rewriting the script for a successful life.

If you want to have more in your life, then you need to start to write a new image in your brain about who you are. "You are a massive success." How does this make you feel? I can tell you the first time I said this I did not believe it. I thought to myself, "Yeah right, Allison, you're hardly a success." Then I questioned why I thought that. What evidence said that I wasn't a massive success? Why could I not think that I already was where I wanted to be?

You have a lot of amazing things to do and achieve, and you need to believe that it will work. You have so much going for you. You have so many people to help. Your strengths and abilities will change the world. They will impact more people than you could ever imagine. Your life will mean something. You are made for greatness. Trust yourself and trust that the universe has your back. Especially when you're doing something new.

For the longest time in my life, I used my logical brain to create all of the reasons why I could not do, be, or have what I wanted in my life. I was an expert at coming up with all of the reasons why it would not work. Then one day I realized that focusing all of my energy on what would not work was causing me to think about lack or scarcity. So I decided to ask myself different questions. One question was, "What if this situation worked better than I could have imagined?"

Do you know what that one question did? It gave me back my power. It helped me realize that my life is in control and that most things will actually turn out better than I could have imagined! Each time I did this, more AWESOME things would happen in my life. As I stopped worrying so much about figuring each step or how I would achieve my goal I found the answers would come to me. I would put a crazy huge goal out there and wait for the resources to present themselves.

I recently received this message from a reader: How do you have such motivation to do so much in life? Do you have any kids? How do you find the time?

To answer the easy part of the questions: Yes,

I have two young children. To find the time? I believe that you need to prioritize the important things in life. I spend a lot of time with our young children because they are my priority. Then on my work days, I am very diligent about prioritizing the things that need to be done. And I am able to fit work into the days I have my kids. Each week I schedule out my time and fit in what is most important.

After reading this question, I wondered: Am I really motivated? Then I realized that I am pretty motivated. But why I am I so motivated? My ability to stay motivated grew out of my life experiences.

At a very young age, I had a relative who was very unmotivated. I saw that he was not helping anyone and made many excuses for what he could not do, rather than what he could do. This propelled me to work as hard as I could at whatever I set my mind to. I read more books than any of my classmates in school. I'd research and write the most complicated report that I could in high school... which my English teacher did NOT appreciate, and I received a B. Interesting side note: The report I wrote was called "The Socioeconomic Status of Children," and it outlined the many challenges that children face when they live in poverty. This report fueled my passion to help our youngest and most vulnerable citizens, our children. One of my first leadership positions was as a director of a non-profit. In this role, I was a voice to state legislators, policymakers, and education leaders for young children by leading a board whose mission was to create early childhood system building. I'm grateful that I started my research in high school to better equip me to advocate for all of the young children in rural Michigan. I was also asked by state leaders to share what we did to grow such a successful collaborative. If I could talk to that English teacher today, I'd say, "I'm okay with the 'B' now!"

When I went off to college, I started in engineering because I knew it would challenge me, and it did. Michigan Technological University is one of the top engineering schools in the nation. General Motors, Ford, Kimberly Clark, Exxon, and many other big companies recruit directly from Michigan Tech for their employees. I started off in engineering and enjoyed learning how engineers thought. But, day after day, week after week, I found I was having to prove myself in every course. I was one of the only female engineering students and I was succeeding. I was on the Dean's list. I was getting really good grades in all of my courses. However, I did not truly enjoy it. If I had been really passionate about engineering, I would have continued, but then I called my cousin who was a female engineer working in corporate America. I asked her if I would have to continue to prove myself in this field every day or if I would be accepted for my intelligence and ability to get the job done. She confirmed my suspicions and told me that she had to prove herself every single day. I also realized that if I became a civil engineer that the bridge problems I was doing in physics classes would be real bridges. This did not thrill me. Thankfully, I made the decision that I did not want to become an engineer. I know people who feel stuck in a career because they got a degree they don't like, then have a career they don't feel satisfied in. I went on to get my Bachelor of Science in Scientific and Technical Communications with a concentration in Engineering. Sounds like a pretty fun and exciting degree right? HA!

I do believe that college did something more for me. At Michigan Tech, I learned how to think like some brilliant people. I learned how to process information like an engineer and communicate really complicated information in a simple way. I realized that I would have to take imperfect action in order to reach success. This has been invaluable to me in creating processes and systems for my businesses. I've learned how to process complicated information and make it simple so people can understand it. One of the best things about what engineers and communicators do is that they solve problems that they do not know answers to. They come up with a problem they want to fix or solve. Then they go through a process to answer it. The engineering process to innovation is amazing. The reason I can type this book on my MacBook Pro is that a team of engineers came up with a problem: People wanted to work on their computers in different locations. How could they design a smaller computer that people could travel with? What would that even look like? Then the engineers designed it! They built the first MacBook and it failed. They took imperfect actions, fixed it, failed, and finally they succeed in creating a laptop that worked. After the computer worked, how would they communicate to people about how awesome this new laptop computer is? How would they create a tribe of awesome, die-hard Apple fans that would keep buying new computers? This is what I learned at college... innovation and creativity.

After I graduated from college, I had an amazing job offer to work at one of the nation's "best places to work" in Texas as a technical writer. It was an awesome honor to be asked. However, after touring the facilities, I turned it down because I had two young siblings at home (Reid and Anika), and my Grandpa Paul Michels was aging. I knew that if I took the job, I would not be able to help them when they needed me. I found myself living in northern Wisconsin with my new husband and unemployed. I was very motivated to find a job. I applied every single day to many jobs. I received more rejection letters than any other person, or at least that is how it felt. I knew that I would be so dedicated to any job that would present itself to me. But none came to me. I wanted to give up. I think it is at these times in life when we want to give up that we have a decision to make. Am I going to "give up" or "go up"? I knew that I was not a person that gave up. I was going to push myself to "go up." My motivation comes from my life experiences.

At age 23, I started my first business: a marketing

firm. The ironic thing is that I had never taken a marketing course in college. Not one. However, I am really good at teaching myself and seeking out resources to learn from. So, that is what I did. I motivated myself to do the best I possibly could for my clients. It worked! I found some amazing clients to work with and felt so blessed to help them market their businesses. I soon was making much more than I would have if I would have gone to Texas. Plus, building my first business helped me learn about building businesses and that laid the foundation for my current businesses. I guess it worked out okay.

In order to believe you can, you need to start with yourself. You need to recognize that you are more than worthy of success. You are exactly the right person to do all of the things that you dream of doing. All of the amazing ideas or goals that you keep having... they are gifts to you. And you are the exact right person to do them. There is not another person on the planet that is like you. You have a unique message, experiences, and personality. That idea or goal is yours to complete. We need you to step up into your greatness. We need you to believe that you can, do, and be anything that you want. We need you to understand that your message counts and will inspire others to step into their greatness.

Finally, remember the hot air balloon effect. You need to fill yourself up with positive energy if you want to move forward. Negative energy drags us down.

Remember: Believe you can and you will!

Practicing the Art of Imperfect Action: Questions to Help You Grow Your Belief to Reach Success

1. **What specifically do I want?** *You need to focus on what you want. Remember, where your focus goes, energy flows. Write out exactly what you want and believe it is achievable.*

2. **Who do I need to help me?** *Find someone to help you. Who has what you want? Could you learn from them? What did they do?*

3. **Why is this a must for me?** *Why do you believe this is so important that you would do anything to achieve it?*

4. **How can I take massive imperfect action?** *Taking the first steps toward your goal is critical to your success. You need to have to*

take action before you can figure out what works and what does not work.

5. **Evaluate the activity and ask, "Am I getting the results I want?"** *The first time you do anything, you are not good at it. To get better, you need to evaluate your results.*

6. **What could I change?** *How could you change your approach to reach success?*

13

what's the next best step?

Your time is limited, so don't waste it living someone else's life. Don't be trapped by dogma—which is living with the results of other people's thinking. Don't let the noise of other's opinions drown out your own inner voice. And most important, have the courage to follow your heart and your intuition. They somehow know what you truly want to become. Everything else is secondary. – Steve Jobs

I started the book with this quote, and I want to revisit it now. After reading this book, you'll likely understand it in a different way. This book was written to empower you to step into your greatness. I hope you feel more self-confident. I hope you know that you are the right person to pursue the goal or dream that keeps popping up in your head. You are the person that needs to step outside of your comfort zone and help others. You are the perfect person to practice the art of imperfect action!

Shortly after my life under construction project, I realized that we don't know how much time we have on this planet. For a long time, I gave myself excuses for why I couldn't pursue my dreams. How many times have you held yourself back from going all in because you think we have more time? Why not do it now? Why not pursue your passions? There are people right now that need you to find your voice or to do whatever it is you are called to do. They need your message exactly the way that you say it. They are struggling in some area of their life and they need you.

Too many people let fear stop them from pursuing their next step. For some reason, the fear of the unknown causes them to not even want to try.

Listen to your Intuition

Trust that you are the person to do that thing you're afraid of doing. – Allison Liddle

Oprah has been teaching me daily. Okay, this is the like the fifth time I've brought this up—have you picked up on the clue yet? You may wonder how I have a successful billionaire teaching me? I've decided that this year I will study her. I'm watching her on YouTube and her channel OWN. I'm reading about her and learning how she thinks.

I have found the key to my success has been to learn from people at a higher level than I am. If I want to have a bigger impact in this world, I need to surround myself with BRILLIANT people. I decided that this year I would choose to have Oprah mentor me. (She doesn't know this yet, but she will when I meet her and thank her for everything she's been teaching me and you.) This morning, Oprah was talking about how when she was a young child her grandmother was a maid in the south. Her grandmother wanted Oprah to also be a maid and work for a nice family. However, Oprah said that her intuition told her that she would do more. She would have a bigger impact and that being a maid would not be her path. She was not sure how or what she would do, but she knew deep within herself that she was destined for greatness.

I'm so grateful that Oprah followed her intuition! WOW! I can't imagine this world without her.

Today, start listening to your intuition. (Hint: it's that little voice inside of you that tells you things.) I've been listening to my intuition more and CRAZY awesome things have happened. It felt really weird at first, but now I enjoy asking my intuition for guidance. Remember, your intuition will help you move forward.

Michael Hyatt said, "Courage is the result of the willingness to act despite our fears." Courage requires you taking the first step toward your goals. Be courageous and brave. Right now you have an opportunity to step into your greatness.

Practice the Art of Imperfect Action

You are now ready to practice the art of imperfect action and get massive results in your life. You're probably really excited because you understand how monumental this is in your life. As we step into our greatness, something magical happens in the way we see the world. It's as if things will start to transpire to your highest good as soon as you truly believe the following:

1. You are enough!
2. You are the exact right person!
3. You need to be you!
4. You have a message that needs to be shared!
5. You already possess everything you need within you!
6. You are guided by God, the universe, or a higher source!

When you understand these things, the people, resources, ideas, solutions, creativity, and innate gifts that you've had all along will suddenly become more apparent to you. You will notice amazing things start to happen. The lack of time that you used to use as an excuse is now abundant. The ideas that were always missing now flow out of you. You will be filled with joy, gratitude, and positive energy because you've found the path that you were meant to be on. You are stepping into your greatness.

The miracles will start to show up in your life almost daily. I'd recommend that each day you look for clues that you are on the right path. They may be messages, quotes, ideas, positive energy, or spurts of intense inspiration. Your next step will show up, and as soon as it does, try to harness it. This miracle of a really great idea needs to be nurtured and protected. Most importantly, it needs you to take imperfect action toward accomplishing it. Your action doesn't need to be huge. Even writing the idea down is an action. Think about it: how many great ideas have you had that you didn't do anything with? What happens to the idea? It likely leaves you and then it's gone forever. If you wrote down the idea, you would have the opportunity to think more about it. You could journal or brainstorm about it. You could even find a close person in your life to discuss it with.

By taking that next best step, you're allowing the universe to guide you. You are looking for clues. You are asking questions. And most importantly, you are being open to the answers because they will likely be different than anything you've ever thought of before. It's important for you to realize that as you step up to be the truest version of yourself, the universe wants you to step fully into your greatness. You need to jump in with both feet. Go all in. Jump, don't step out of your comfort zone. Take the risk. Fail, learn, and grow. Be brave and courageous. The world needs you to become all that you were meant to be. You need to 'BE YOU.' Remember there are people today that are waiting for you to find your voice and to start practicing the art of imperfect action. By stepping into who you truly are, you will change their lives. As soon as you decide to feed your faith, rather than feeding your fear, the universe knows and wants to support you. All success comes from daring to begin!

Ask yourself, "What's the next best step?"

Remember: Commit to your dreams, be courageous, and take imperfect action!

acknowledgments

The Art of Imperfect Action: All Success Comes from Daring to Begin was definitely a big project and I thank everyone in my life that supported creating it. I may have written the words, but each of you impacted my heart and that's the true gift.

I thank my super loving and supportive husband, Tony. You're sweet and kind and help me so much every day to stay motivated, remain focused, and believe in my huge goals. I can't imagine doing this life with anyone other than you.

A huge thank you to my awesome kiddos, Avery and Logan. I love you both so much. I'm proud of your compassion, leadership, and kindness. You make this world a better place.

I thank my mom Shari, my stepfather Rick, my

sister Anika, and my brother Reid for their love and support each day. Mom, you were the reason I started to practice the art of imperfect action and believe that I truly can help people. Anika, thank you for being the best sister ever and for helping behind the scenes with my books. Reid, thank you for always being supportive of me and willing to design something for me or kick around ideas. Mr. Parks thank you for teaching me about leadership. Love you all!

I thank all of my GREAT family for being loving, kind, and teaching me so many life lessons. I'm grateful to all of you.

I thank all my AMAZING mentors for teaching me so much and coming into my life at just the right time. John C. Maxwell, Paul Martinelli, Mark Cole, Chris Robinson, Jeff Rose, Ria Story, Roddy Galbraith, Christian Simpson, Deb Eslinger, Kellie George, and of course, Clifton Maclin, —I owe you each my gratitude for your willingness to pour into me with your wisdom.

Thank you to the amazing authors who graciously gave their permission to have excerpts of their work included in *The Art of Imperfect Action*:

- Gloria J. Burgess, PhD | CEO & Founder, Jazz International | Executive Director & Founder, The Lift Every Voice Foundation and author of *Paraguay's Landfill Harmonic Orchestra Success*
- Barbara Gustavson, President & Executive Coach, Discover Next Step, Executive Director, John Maxwell Team, DiscoverNextStep.com and author of *Understanding Success Is Not All Or Nothing*
- Paul Martinelli, President of The John Maxwell Team and author of the presentation *The 5 Mistakes of Goal Setting*
- Sid Samuels, owner of the commercial construction contractor group Samuels Group, Inc., www.samuelsgroup.net and author of the *Roller Coaster Effect*
- Timothy Teasdale, Director, Transformacion Paraguay, www.transformacion.org and author of *What Does Success Mean in Transforming a Country?*

Thank you to Rochelle Melander and Sherry Larson, my editors. I appreciate everything you did to help create this book. I thank my proofreader, Danielle Anderson, for her keen eye (again!). And I thank all of the people who offered their insights as I navigated through the book-publishing process, especially everyone that contributed to my testimonials, my book launch team, and wonderful friends who keep pushing me to write, create, speak, and pursue my passions. THANK YOU!!!!

To my readers, I thank all of you for reading this book and supporting my CRAZY huge goals. God bless!

about allison
liddle

Allison Liddle is a bestselling author of *Life Under Construction: Designing a Life You Love*. She is a certified John Maxwell Team keynote speaker, executive coach, and leadership trainer who is passionate about helping people thrive both personally and professionally. As an entrepreneur, she started her first business at age twenty-three. She then went on to found a national, award-winning financial planning firm called Prosper Wealth Management that has been featured in *Forbes* and *USA Today*. Allison is a lifelong Wisconsin resident; she currently lives in central Wisconsin with her family. *The Art of Imperfect Action* is her second book. You can visit her at www.allisonliddle.com.

works cited

Buffet, W. (2010, 6 16). *Warren Buffett Pledge Letter.* Retrieved from CNN: https://money.cnn.com/2010/06/15/news/newsmakers/Warren_Buffett_Pledge_Letter.fortune/index.htm

Gates Foundation. (2017, 12 31). *Gates Foundation Factsheet.* Retrieved from https://www.gatesfoundation.org/Who-We-Are/General-Information/Foundation-Factsheet

Kruse, K. (2016, 8 2). *The 80/20 Rule And How It Can Change Your Life.* Retrieved 2018, from Forbes: https://www.forbes.com/sites/kevinkruse/2016/03/07/80-20-rule/#18b429573814

Marksberry, K. (2018, 8 24). *Take a Deep Breath.* Retrieved from THE AMERICAN INSTITUTE OF STRESS: https://www.stress.org/take-a-deep-breath/

Maxwell Maltz, M. (2015). *Psycho Cybernetics.* TargerPerigee.

Maxwell, J. (2018, 8 2). Retrieved from John

Maxwell Blog: http://www.success.com/article/
john-c-maxwell-6-tips-to-develop-and-model-an-
abundance-mindset

Merriam Webster . (2018, 8 11). *Goal.* Retrieved
from Merriam Webster: https://www.merriam-
webster.com/dictionary/goal

Newton's third law. (2018, 8 2). *Newtons third law.*
Retrieved from Physics Classroom:
http://www.physicsclassroom.com/class/
newtlaws/Lesson-4/Newton-s-Third-Law

Organization, W. H. (2018). *Preterm birth.*
website: (http://www.who.int/news-room/fact-
sheets/detail/preterm-birth).

Positive Psychology Program. (2017, 2 28). *What
is Gratitude and What Is Its Role in Positive
Psychology?* Retrieved from Positive Psychology
Program:
https://positivepsychologyprogram.com/
gratitude-appreciation/

Shapiro, E. a. (2010, 4 30). *Overcoming F.E.A.R.:
False Evidence Appearing Real .* Retrieved from
Oprah: http://www.oprah.com/spirit/transform-
your-fear-into-courage/all

The American Institute of Stress. (2014, 7 8).
Daily Life. Retrieved from The American Institute
of Stress: https://www.stress.org/daily-life/

Winfrey, O. (2013, 5 30). *Oprah Winfrey Harvard Commencement speech | Harvard Commencement 2013*. Retrieved from Youtube: https://www.youtube.com/ watch?v=mc3Y5S7m2XM

Winfrey, O. (2015, 8 5). *How to Separate the Voice in Your Head from the Real You | SuperSoul Sunday | OWN*. Retrieved from https://www.youtube.com/ watch?v=3el1Kp7clsA&t=0s&list=PLH8QAEeOR3qGPnNMfrvK hs&index=13

Workman Publishing . (2015). *You Are Doing a Freaking Great Job.: And Other Reminders of Your Awesomeness*. Workman Publishing.

Made in the USA
Columbia, SC
10 March 2019